P9-CAM-486

# Summary of Contents

# SCRUM: NOVICE
# TO NINJA

BY M. DAVID GREEN

# Scrum: Novice to Ninja

by M. David Green

Copyright © 2016 SitePoint Pty. Ltd.

**Product Manager**: Simon Mackie     **Cover Designer**: Alex Walker

**Technical Reviewer**: David Shirey     **Illustrator**: Natalia Balska

**English Editor**: Ralph Mason     **Author Photograph**: Khaled Sayed

## Notice of Rights

## Notice of Liability

## Trademark Notice

Published by SitePoint Pty. Ltd.

48 Cambridge Street Collingwood
VIC Australia 3066
Web: www.sitepoint.com
Email: business@sitepoint.com

ISBN 978-0-9943469-1-9 (print)

ISBN 978-0-9943469-9-5 (ebook)
Printed and bound in the United States of America

## About M. David Green

M. David Green is a writer and agile business coach, and the founder of Agile That Works (http://www.agilethatworks.com), a consultancy that helps people in engineering organizations collaborate to make constant improvement a daily practice.

David studied Anthropology and Sociology at UC Berkeley, and later earned his MBA in Organizational Behavior. He has worked as an engineer, a writer, a designer, a marketing director, and a communications analyst in companies from Fortune 100 giants to tiny high-tech startups in San Francisco and Silicon Valley. He also teaches engineering techniques and agile principles through SitePoint.

With over 10,000 hours of experience on scrum teams under his belt, David enjoys sharing what he's seen to watch others improve their processes. Now he consults with companies to help them apply scrum and agile practices to improve productivity, communication, flexibility, and quality of life for engineers and the people who work with them.

## About SitePoint

SitePoint specializes in publishing fun, practical, and easy-to-understand content for web professionals. Visit http://www.sitepoint.com/ to access our blogs, books, newsletters, articles, and community forums. You'll find a stack of information on JavaScript, PHP, Ruby, mobile development, design, and more.

*This book is dedicated to my husband, who reminds me every day what truly matters.*

# Table of Contents

# Preface

If you haven't heard about scrum, and you work in web or mobile development, it's time you did. Scrum is a way of organizing engineering teams around time-tested techniques to improve communication, increase the flexibility of the product development process, support constant improvement, and provide a sustainable rhythm for productivity with less pain and more participation.

Scrum offers a core set of operating principles, and supports incredible flexibility for a team to adapt the process to their particular needs. Properly applied, scrum insulates engineers against interruptions and micromanagement while giving product managers the flexibility to adapt to market changes regularly, and the ability to predict how much work the team can take on and complete.

In this book, you will be introduced to the fundamentals of scrum, and given examples that you can apply immediately. And since scrum is as much about the people as it is about the processes, we will introduce you to a typical web and mobile development team, and show you the impact of scrum on their jobs, their working relationships, and the things they care about most in their professions.

Whether you're not sure what scrum is, or you think your scrum process isn't all that it should be, this book can help. Scrum isn't magic, but the results it can produce are well worth taking the time to learn how to apply it effectively.

## Who Should Read This Book

This book is for anyone who works in a team to build web or mobile apps: engineers, QA, management, designers, and product managers. It assumes no familiarity with scrum or other project management techniques. While it's aimed at readers who have little understanding of scrum, it will also be useful to those who are currently using scrum, but aren't sure that they're getting the results that they want from it.

## Conventions Used

You'll notice that we've used certain typographic and layout styles throughout this book to signify different types of information. Look out for the following items.

## Tips, Notes, and Warnings

### Hey, You!

Tips provide helpful little pointers.

### Ahem, Excuse Me ...

Notes are useful asides that are related—but not critical—to the topic at hand. Think of them as extra tidbits of information.

### Make Sure You Always ...

... pay attention to these important points.

### Watch Out!

Warnings highlight any gotchas that are likely to trip you up along the way.

# Supplementary Materials

**https://www.sitepoint.com/premium/books/scrum1**
The book's website, containing links, updates, resources, and more.

**http://community.sitepoint.com/**
SitePoint's forums, for help on any tricky web problems.

**books@sitepoint.com**
Our email address, should you need to contact us for support, to report a problem, or for any other reason.

# Want to take your learning further?

Thanks for choosing to buy a SitePoint book. Would you like to continue learning? You can now gain unlimited access to ALL SitePoint books and courses plus high-quality books from our selected partners at SitePoint Premium[1]. Enroll now and start learning today!

---

[1] https://www.sitepoint.com/premium/home

# Chapter 1

# Introducing Scrum

## What Is Scrum?

If you picked up this book to learn about applying scrum to your web or mobile development team, you may already be familiar with the terms scrum and agile. Perhaps you received this book from your company, or maybe you've been tasked with implementing an agile process in your own organization. Whatever the reason, it's always useful to start with a clear, shared definition of the relevant terms.

**Scrum** is one of several techniques for managing product development organizations, lumped under the broad category of agile software development. **Agile** approaches are designed to support iterative, flexible, and sustainable methods for running a product engineering organization.

Among the various agile techniques, scrum is particularly well suited to the types of organizations that develop products such as websites and mobile software. The focus on developing cohesive, modular, measurable features that can be estimated relatively, tracked easily, and that may need to adapt quickly to changing market conditions makes scrum particularly appropriate for these types of projects.

Scrum encourages teams to work in a focused way for a limited period of time on a clearly defined set of features, understanding that the next set of features they may be asked to work on could be unpredictable because of changes in the marketplace, feedback from customers, or any number of factors. Scrum allows teams to develop an improved ability to estimate how much effort it will take to produce a new feature in a relative way, based on the work involved in features they've developed before. And scrum creates the opportunity for a team to reflect on the process and improve it regularly, bringing everybody's feedback into play.

 **Don't Confuse Merely Applying Scrum Terms with Actually Using Scrum**

A familiar anti-pattern in non-agile organizations looking to mask their process problems is using the terminology of scrum as a labeling system on top of their waterfall techniques and tools. That can create confusion, and even negative associations among people who have seen these terms used incorrectly, and who mistakenly believe they've seen scrum in action.

As we go through this book, you're going to find out more about how scrum functions. You're going to be introduced to all of the aspects of scrum, including its rituals, its artifacts, and the roles that it creates for the people in an organization. We're going to introduce you to a team of people working in a scrum environment, and show you how they adopted scrum in the first place, and how they adapted to it.

Before we get there, it's worthwhile taking a moment to position scrum in its historical context. After all, scrum isn't the only way to organize product development. Scrum came into existence right around the time that web development emerged on the engineering landscape, and it flourished as mobile technology became part of our daily lives. If you consider how scrum works, where it came from, and how we apply it, I think you'll see that there might be a reason for that.

 **Scrum's Odd Vocabulary**

The vocabulary of scrum is distinctive, and may sound odd. That's intentional. Scrum uses terms such as ritual, artifact, and story to make it clear that these concepts are different from related ideas that may be encountered in other project management approaches.

# A Brief History of Scrum

The original concept for scrum came out of Japan, introduced in 1986 as part of *The New Product Development Game* by Hirotaka Takeuchi and Ikujiro Nonaka. They applied the concept of a scrum, taken from the team game rugby, to describe cross-functional team organization based around moving forward in a layered approach.

Their concepts were codified as the Scrum Methodology at a joint presentation in 1995 by Ken Schwaber and Jeff Sutherland, based on their personal experiences applying the concepts in their own organizations. This work inspired the 2001 book, *Agile Software Development with Scrum*, written by Schwaber and Mike Beedle.

At the time, the most prevalent approach for software development was called the **waterfall model**. Under the waterfall model, product development happens in stages, leading sequentially from requirements through design, implementation, and release. Until the 1990s, most software development was targeted at packaged software delivery for desktop computers. Such products had long development and release cycles. While waterfall is well-suited to products that have a long development trajectory, it doesn't adapt well to situations where the product needs to change constantly in response to changing conditions.

In the mid-to-late 1990s, new publishing models emerged involving electronic media and the Internet. To support these, software development organizations had to incorporate more flexibility to adapt to changing browsers, tight media deadlines, and a variety of platforms with different requirements. Soon after that, the development of large monolithic software applications that lived on desktop computers gave way to smaller, more nimble apps that were delivered through mobile devices. A different approach was needed for developing these.

It isn't a coincidence that agile approaches became codified, and quickly became popular, just as the marketplace was shifting from desktop software to web and mobile software.

# Comparing Scrum and Waterfall

The slow cycle of waterfall development may still be appropriate in a world of hardware development, or even in gaming. These industries rely on long, stable markets, where many of the decisions are either repetitive, constrained by external resources, or need to be made far in advance because of the massive scale and expense of development.

Web and mobile technology moves too fast for a waterfall approach. By the time you're done developing a solution to one problem and gathering feedback from users, the technology has already moved on, and you may have a very small window of opportunity to capitalize on your solution.

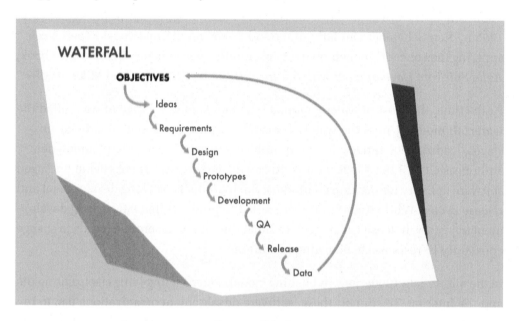

Figure 1.1. Waterfall

In a waterfall approach, the ideas for what needs to be developed may come from customers, from the executives, from market research, or from the imagination of people making the decisions and setting the budgets. Those ideas are passed on to product managers, who create a long product roadmap. They establish and collect requirements, write out classic product requirement documents, and then pass those requirements on to designers to create prototypes as wireframes and mockups. Those prototypes are passed on to an engineering team that implements those ideas, and produces a product that can finally be released to the marketplace. Until that product is released and put in the hands of customers, no feedback into the process is generated.

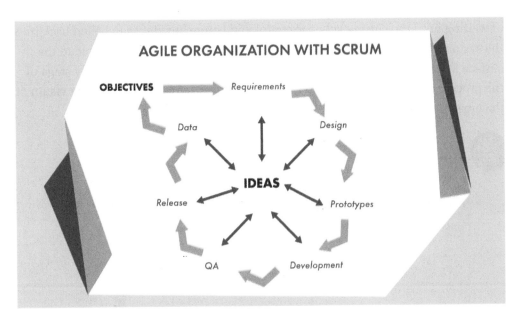

Figure 1.2. Agile Organization

In an agile organization, guiding objectives and key performance indicators guide the process, but the team manages itself to meet those objectives. A product owner maintains the overall vision, and works with the scrum master to make sure that everyone on the team is clear about the objectives and how they'll be measured. The input of the designers and the engineers is included at every stage in this process. Features are conceived and formulated into stories when the team is ready to work on them. No idea gets locked into a static product timeline.

The value to a company of hiring its own team of designers and engineers is that these people can bring their design thinking and their current technical knowledge to the table for the benefit of the organization's own objectives. Designers should be evaluating the user experience and figuring out the best solutions to real customers' problems, not decorating bad ideas to make them functional.

Getting engineers involved in ideation allows them to pull in the latest technology as early as possible, since they're in the best position to know what's technically feasible. The sooner the designers and engineers are brought into the planning process, the more agile development will be.

Scrum allows the full resources of the team to be applied when and where they can do the most good, and to work together in a sustainable and productive way. Instead of waiting until the entire cycle has completed before any data can be fed back into the system, ideas are generated at every stage, and encouraged to bubble to the surface at the end of each sprint. Total participation of the team in every stage of the process allows these ideas to feed into the objectives, and support the vision of the organization.

### Mixing Scrum With Waterfall

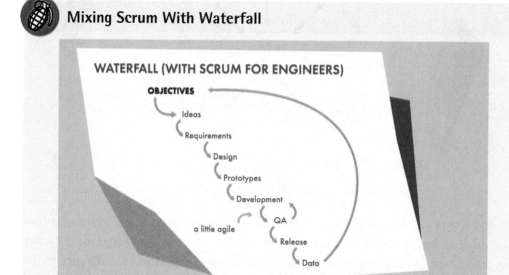

Figure 1.3. Waterfall (With Scrum for Engineering)

While some organizations may claim to follow scrum, many of them actually follow a modified waterfall approach, using scrum techniques only for development. The rest of the organization structures itself around long-lived product timelines with static objectives. While that may be an improvement over pure waterfall, in that it allows the engineers to iterate and improve their process, it doesn't take full advantage of the potential of scrum. Isolating scrum inside the development loop without inviting the learnings of the team into the planning and market testing process is a waste of resources, and a wasted opportunity.

Mixing a little scrum into an otherwise waterfall organization is usually not a good idea, since it can draw attention to the fundamental conflicts between the different approaches, and foster friction.

# Reasons to Choose Scrum for Web and Mobile

We've covered how scrum works, and why it's a productive way to structure web and mobile product development. At this point, it's worth taking a moment to recap some of the highlights of how scrum applies in particular to web and mobile product development.

Fundamentally, scrum offers a team-based approach to project work that allows a product development process to benefit from iterative self-reflection, helps a team learn how to estimate their own ability to address unfamiliar tasks, exposes metrics about team effectiveness, encourages dialogue about feature implementation instead of static specifications, and supports rapid response to changing market conditions in a sustainable manner.

All of those advantages can make a real difference when doing web and mobile development. Most work in web or mobile development tends to be very time sensitive, and needs to respond quickly to changes in the marketplace. Whether that means new browsers, new technologies, or new messaging that needs to be communicated immediately, web and mobile teams have to be able to respond quickly.

Scrum provides a framework that allows developers to work toward a vision, and the opportunity to shift direction as the environment changes without feeling torn away from their focus.

When following best development practices, the type of work that's involved in building and enhancing a web or mobile project tends to break down into discrete pieces that can be worked on independently, with a core of infrastructure stories that support a broad range of independent feature stories. This makes it easier for one part of a web or mobile project to be developed in isolation, and leverage the shared resources of other parts of the same project.

Scrum encourages teams to spell out the work on a new feature so that it can be developed in parallel, without relying on other undeveloped features. By using stories, and making sure each story is properly formatted and estimated, the team sets itself up for a consistent and productive development experience.

## Some Scrum Terms Defined

When scrum uses a word, it means just what scrum chooses for it to mean. But unlike Humpty Dumpty in *Through the Looking Glass*, scrum relies on familiar and easily understood definitions. Learning the language is one of the first steps in acquiring a new skill, and consistent use of language is fundamental to teams trying to work together. The terms below are only some of the ones that will be defined in much more detail later in the book, but a brief glance through these concepts may help as you read on.

| | |
|---|---|
| **Agile** | a set of software development practices designed to help engineers work together and adapt to changes quickly and easily. |
| **Artifact** | a physical or virtual tool used by a scrum team to facilitate the scrum process |
| **Blocker** | anything keeping an engineer from moving forward on a task in progress |
| **Customer** | whoever has engaged the team to create a product |
| **Engineer/Developer** | a person responsible for creating and maintaining the technology that goes into a product |
| **Engineering Organization** | the part of a company where engineers are employed to create and maintain products |
| **Product** | what the engineering organization is building or maintaining for a customer |
| **Product backlog** | a constantly evolving list of potential features or changes for a product |
| **Product owner** | a person who helps define the product for the team, and whose job may be on the line if the customer isn't satisfied |
| **Retrospective** | a regular opportunity for the team to reflect on how they are doing, and what they could do better |

| | |
|---|---|
| **Ritual** | a group of people coming together as part of the scrum process for a fixed time, with a specified agenda, to achieve a clearly defined outcome |
| **Scrum Master** | a person responsible for maintaining the artifacts and overseeing the rituals of scrum |
| **Sprint** | a fixed number of days during which the team can work together to produce an agreed upon set of changes to the product |
| **Sprint backlog** | a finite and well-defined set of stories the team has agreed they can reasonably complete in the current sprint |
| **Story** | a clear and consistent way of chunking, phrasing, and discussing work the team may need to do on the product |
| **User** | a person who will be making use of the product |

Scrum is also flexible enough to support working styles for product owners who prefer to break down stories that can be completed in one week, two weeks, three weeks, four weeks or longer. While most web and mobile development teams tend to split the work into one- or two-week segments—known in scrum terminology as sprints—whatever the team agrees on should work. As long as the team is keeping track of how they work together, and they're given the opportunity to reflect on a regular basis about their schedules, scrum can adapt to work on projects ranging from the simplest to the most complex.

## Time Sensitivity

Scrum provides opportunities in every sprint to integrate the ideas of designers, engineers, executives, customers, product managers, and customers through real customer data. Because of the cyclical nature of scrum, and the iterative approach that encourages learning as you go, scrum allows mobile and web projects to adapt to changing technologies and changing market expectations quickly.

# Modular Development

Scrum supports the ability to develop a project in modules. Because scrum is based on thinking in terms of slices of functionality, it's perfectly suited for making independent, interoperable features that can be developed atomically and work together harmoniously.

For example, a new section for a website may inherit styling from a shared style guide and CSS structure, and may inherit its functionality from a shared template. The work to build out that section relies on those other components remaining static long enough to complete the work. Scrum provides the stability to support that, without limiting the development of the rest of the site.

At the same time, updating the infrastructure of a product to support a new feature may happen at any time in the process, so a team has to consider up front how to make those changes safely, without breaking the work being done on other features.

As another example, sometimes an API that every feature of the site relies on needs to be changed. Scrum encourages the team to manage the code in a modular, testable way, so that changes can be inherited by other feature stories that might be in progress without undue breakage.

# Flexible Scheduling

Companies serving customers in the web and mobile space need to be able to respond quickly to changes. However, engineers need to be confident that what they're working on isn't going to change before they can get the feature developed. It can be difficult to balance those two objectives.

Scrum provides windows of opportunity that are long enough to allow a web or mobile feature to be fully developed, while still allowing a product to change directions at the end of each sprint, based on data from the marketplace.

# Reflection and Improvement

A scrum team isn't only looking to improve the product: they're also looking to improve their own process. Scrum teams get better over time at estimating how much work they can do, and improving their approach to working so that they can be the most productive.

By giving the team the opportunity to look at its own process, and figure out how it works best together, scrum makes maximum use of the limited resources of any organization.

## Summary

That was a quick overview of scrum, taken from a 30,000-foot perspective. We had a brief introduction to how scrum works, and why it can be effective for certain types of product development. We contrasted scrum with the more traditional waterfall approach for software development, and discussed why it emerged when it did. We also noted how well suited scrum is for web and mobile development projects.

But scrum isn't just an abstract concept and a bunch of unfamiliar buzzwords. Scrum is a practical and flexible approach to product development that relies on the active and engaged participation of real people. So in the next chapter, we're going to meet a few of the typical people who might work in a web or mobile development organization. We'll talk to them about some of their frustrations, find out what they hope to get out of scrum, and ask them about their concerns when they consider scrum.

As we go through this book, keep these people in mind. We'll be meeting them again, and following them through their process as they learn and start to apply scrum to their work.

# Meet the Team

Scrum is about how a team works together, so it's important to start with who the team is. Who are the people involved in a typical web or mobile development project, and what do they anticipate when they think of scrum?

We're going to be introduced to a few typical players in a web and mobile development project. The team we'll meet works at a fictional meme publishing company, on a service called WithKittens.com—an engine to add kittens to images on websites.

Each of the people working on WithKittens.com has objectives and problems that center around their part in delivering this critical service to their free-tier B2C and enterprise-class B2E customers. The jobs they hold in the WithKittens organization describe the skills and experience they have, and how they're positioned in the hierarchy of the company—two factors that are independent of scrum.

Some of the people we'll meet will include:

- Engineers (senior and junior)

- Team Managers

- QA Engineers

- Product Managers

- Designers

To help get into their heads, we'll ask a representative from each of these groups to answer a series of questions. We want to find out how they view their place in the organization, their motivations, their frustrations, their perfect day, and the biggest concerns they have about scrum.

 **These Are Hypothetical People**

Of course, there's no such thing as a universal engineer, designer, or manager. But you may see patterns in these responses that are likely to repeat themselves on different web and mobile development teams.

# A Senior Engineer

## My Role

I need to take the lead in being responsible for the development of WithKittens.com. I not only have to do the work, but also have to keep track of all the variables that can stop the work from happening. I'm a specialist in developing the custom Kittens API, but I also have to understand how the whole stack comes together. Frequently, I'm the first person contacted when a problem comes up, and may be the only one who knows how to solve that problem.

## Motivations

I have the experience to know when the project is moving in the right direction, and what issues we need to watch out for. I want to see the code improve as it develops, while still supporting the requirements of the project. My goal is to make the product adhere to the highest practical technical standards. I got my title because I have years of experience, including work on projects that went far off the rails, and I never want to see that happen again.

## Perfect Day

The perfect day for me is uninterrupted time to work on my part of the code. I usually know what I need to do next, and I don't want to be interrupted. I don't want surprises. I got to this point in my career because I have the talent and the knowledge to do the work and do it right. I like to work with other people who can bounce ideas around and discuss technical issues at the same level that I can. But, while not wanting to sound like a curmudgeon, I really just want everyone to get out of my way and let me do my job.

## Frustrations

Because I'm one of the most experienced members of the team, I'm often the first one asked when problems come up around the Kittens API. My experience with this part of the system means that I'm sometimes the only one who can find answers to these problems. I don't mind showing people how to do something if they're interested, but usually the ones asking the questions don't understand things as well as I do, so I may need to explain the same thing over and over. Being interrupted in the middle of working on something difficult, or being asked to go to a meeting where my expertise isn't actually required, are two of my leading frustrations.

## Concerns About Scrum

I've been on multiple teams that have claimed to be following scrum. I don't know what they were doing, but I hope real scrum isn't like that. We always seemed to have dozens of meetings that never ended, and requirements that changed all the time. They threw around words like "transparency" when they really meant "micro-management". I never had the opportunity to focus on the long-term objectives of the project before things changed again. Instead, we just got into endless debates about the process that interfered with getting the work done. You could say I'm pretty skeptical about scrum.

# A Junior Engineer

## My Role

I was brought in to do performance optimizations on the front end, but the way it's worked out, I seem to do a lot of styling and layout fixes for WithKittens.com's membership and admin pages. I've kind of become the one they call when there's a bug that needs to be fixed, and nobody else wants to work on it. I can usually figure it out, even if it takes me a little bit longer than it might've taken some of the more seasoned people. I guess that makes sense. This is only my second job, and I've only been here about six months. I'm still learning.

## Motivations

I got into engineering because I love working with computers. I was really excited when they gave me the opportunity to work on WithKittens.com, because it's a very popular site. It's the sort of thing that will look good on my resume. I'd like to do some projects that I can be proud of. And really, I want to learn from the other engineers. Sometimes I'm amazed at how much talent there is around here, and I'm just wondering when I'm going to feel like I have the same skill set as these other people.

## Perfect Day

Most days start with finishing up the things I was doing the day before. I usually have a pretty long list of tasks that need to get done. They pile a lot onto my plate, and I just go through the list and try to do one at a time until I'm finished. On a good day, I can finish four or five tasks and get them into review before everyone else goes home. On a bad day, I might find myself grinding on the same task for hours into the evening. But even those are good days in a way. Days like that give me an opportunity to learn some more about the code behind WithKittens.com. All in all, I like what I'm doing.

## Frustrations

I think my biggest frustration is that I feel like an imposter. Sometimes I can't believe they gave me this job. The people I work with seem so much more experienced, and they have such fast answers to questions that I wouldn't have any idea how to answer. I don't have a lot of experience working at different companies, and as far as I can tell, most of the people who work here are pretty satisfied with the work, so I don't complain about the long hours. I just wish I had an opportunity to do more than the small tasks they assign me. Sometimes it feels as if I'm trapped in a CSS ghetto, when I know I could do more if given the opportunity.

## Concerns About Scrum

I've read a little bit about scrum, and I'm curious what it's going to feel like when we start doing it. Right now we have a routine that works. I know what I'm expected to do, and as long as I get my work done, everything goes pretty smoothly. I hear that in scrum there's a lot of talking. I'm not a big talker. I tend to like to sit quietly and get my work done, and I don't feel as if I know enough to have a lot of opinions worth sharing. I'm a little bit concerned that scrum is going to put a spotlight on me, and force me out of my shell more than I'm comfortable with.

# An Engineering Manager

## My Role

I started here at WithKittens.com as a senior engineer. I was promoted to manager here after the last manager left. As the manager, I'm responsible for making sure that my team has everything they need, and that everybody is working on what they should be working on. I report up to senior management, and have to justify the budget for the team, and provide reports that demonstrate that we're doing what the company needs us to be doing. Sometimes I have to play referee, and sometimes I have to make some tough decisions. That goes with the job. It's not as much fun as being an engineer, but it seemed like a good opportunity for advancement at the time.

## Motivations

I really like my team. I hired about half of them, and the others were mostly working here when I got here. I like to think that what I do, I do for them. My job is to keep everybody engaged, employed, and content. At the same time, I have some strong opinions about how the code should evolve, and I like to make sure my influence is in there. At heart, I'm an engineer, and I like working with talented engineers.

## Perfect Day

My best days are the quietest ones. As the manager, I'm often called on to solve problems to do with organizational, administrative, and even sometimes human resource issues. I enjoy the opportunity to do one-on-one meetings with my team members, and I try to schedule these around the workload. Most days start and end by looking at an overview of what everybody on the team is working on, so I can make sure the work is being distributed evenly. Sometimes that's both an art and a science.

## Frustrations

As the manager, I'm responsible for all staffing and budget decisions in the team. I decide how the budget gets spent, and I have to make sure enough budget is provided to keep the team supplied with everything they need to do their jobs. Sometimes it feels as if I spend half my time justifying the budget to senior management, and the other half explaining why we don't have enough budget to do something everybody knows we should be doing. The responsibilities of management also involve dealing with interpersonal issues. Human resources can publish all the memos they like, but there's no manual for figuring out how to get people to work together peacefully.

## Concerns About Scrum

The way I keep hearing scrum described, they talk about self-managing teams. That concerns me a little bit. After all, my role on the team is managing. I don't like to think of some new process coming in and bypassing my authority. I don't have a clear picture of what a manager does in scrum. A lot of the things I've read talk about scrum Masters, product owners, and team members. They don't talk about how the manager fits in.

# A QA Engineer

## My Role

There's a lot of technical complexity behind a site like WithKittens.com. As a quality assurance engineer, I need to be aware of all the site's specifications and test every aspect of the site to make sure nothing breaks as the code evolves. That means building a complex and comprehensive suite of tests whenever there's a new feature, and making sure every one of those tests passes every time the code changes. My job is very detail oriented. I rely on some testing tools that nobody else in the department has any idea how to work. But they don't have to, as long as I'm here.

## Motivations

Sometimes I feel as if I'm motivated by little green dots on my screen. When I run my test suite, and I see that every single test is passing, there's a sense of satisfaction.

But it's also very satisfying to find those elusive little bugs that nobody else saw. I try to look at every specification for new product feature, and figure out the edge cases that nobody else is going to test. For example, if a user is supposed to enter a number into a field on a form, I find out what happens if they enter a negative number, or a word, or submit the form without any data. If I'm doing my job well, I'm keeping the engineers on their toes, and making sure they write code that's resilient.

## Perfect Day

I like it best when I have a well-defined project to test, and I'm building up a set of tests that need to be run. I take the code, I run the tests, and if anything fails I write the report and let the engineers know. It's interesting and challenging work, writing tests that address all of the possible concerns when a new feature is being developed. Having the time to break apart a new feature, work out what the edge cases are, and build a test suite that's very robust and comprehensive makes me feel like I'm doing my job.

## Frustrations

As the one who reports when there are problems with the code, sometimes I feel as if I'm the bearer of bad news. My work comes at the end of the process, after the engineer has completed everything. Often I need to get answers from the engineers about how they developed the code in order to test it properly. It's frustrating when they've moved on to the next assignment, and they don't have time to get back to me with the information I need. I also get pressured to do my work very quickly when there's a deadline to be met. That means some bugs I might have caught can get through.

## Concerns About Scrum

I'm not sure if scrum has anything to do with me. Most of what I read about scrum has to do with how the code gets developed, not how it gets tested. I'm open to the idea of working in a scrum environment, but my role as a QA engineer doesn't translate to the kind of work the rest of the engineers are doing on the team. The QA structure here at WithKittens.com involves me reporting to the manager of QA, not the manager of the engineering team. I'm not sure how I'm going to fit in.

# A Product Manager

## My Role

As the product manager for the WithKittens.com site, I work for the Product group, which reports up to the CEO. We're responsible for making sure the services we provide to our customers are the best they can possibly be. I have to balance a lot of concerns, including feature requirements from Sales, promises that the executives make to the board of directors and the investors, as well as practical budgeting and engineering requirements. At the same time, I have to be looking at how the product is evolving, and planning for the next release and the next version. Our site needs to continue to support all of our existing users, while growing to reach new users.

## Motivations

What gets me most excited about my work is the opportunity to build a service that exceeds the expectations of our customers. I'm happy when I get an email from a user who's received superior service from us. But email isn't the only way I find out about that. I love to see our numbers improve over time. We've incorporated a lot of different tracking services into our site, so we can measure where people are getting the most use out of what we provide. Beyond that, one of my favorite responsibilities is user testing, where I can sit down with customers and find out what they like about our service, and where they think we need to improve. Ultimately, it's about providing the best service we possibly can, and I enjoy being a part of that.

## Perfect Day

A typical day for me goes back and forth between work with the designers on new features, work with clients on expectations, work with executives on feature expectations, and work with the engineers on how those features are being developed. I enjoy the opportunity to see a project from so many perspectives simultaneously, but I have to switch gears frequently, sometimes thinking about what's going to come down the road, and sometimes thinking about what's happening right now. I spend a lot of my time in meetings. When I'm not in a meeting, I'm usually writing reports or specifications based on design, testing, and research.

## Frustrations

Have you ever heard the old saying, "The plan is worthless, but planning is invaluable"? Sometimes that describes my life. I can spend weeks building up the perfect set of specifications for the next iteration of WithKittens.com, only to have everything pulled apart by one rejection from engineering due to practicality, or one comment from executives about a feature we never imagined before. Sometimes my job feels like building a ship in a bottle. I have to drive forward my vision of where I need the products to go, but I can't actually touch the pieces. I also have to deal with the fact that my schedule isn't as mission-critical as the dedicated time of a designer or an engineer. As a product manager, I need to make myself available when the resources I have to work with are available, not the other way around.

## Concerns About Scrum

My biggest concern about scrum is the way it doesn't seem to address deadlines. I live in the real world, and that means sometimes you have to promise something will be delivered on a certain date. Sometimes you have to be very specific about what that thing is going to be. Scrum seems to take deadlines and product specifications pretty loosely, allowing the agile process to define them instead of the other way around. I like the idea that a team following scrum will get better at estimating their time, so that I can get a sense upfront how long something we need will take. I don't like the idea that we may not know for sure what we're going to deliver at a specific time. I know the people I have to deal with, and getting them used to that kind of uncertainty might be difficult.

# A Designer

## My Role

Design is a discipline that reaches into the very depths of a product. I try to design the product from the inside out, thinking about what users expect, and how we can meet and exceed those expectations. That means I have to think both visually and experientially at the same time. Of course, I'm responsible for the style guide and maintaining visual consistency. But I'm also responsible for making sure there's functional consistency. When users come to WithKittens.com, it's my responsibility to make sure they know what they're supposed to do next. If I'm doing my job right, the designs I provide to the team explain both how users are going to flow through the site, and what their experience is going to look like along the way.

## Motivations

I know I can be a little bit obsessive sometimes, but it gives me a strong sense of satisfaction to move through a site I've designed and feel that there's a holistic consistency to the visuals as well as the flow. I want the work I produce to give users an experience that makes sense, that's enjoyable, and that fulfills the potential of the product. For a site like WithKittens.com, we have a number of design objectives around keeping the user experience playful, inspiring, and humorous. It's important to me that the work I do stays true to those design objectives. I don't mind fighting for what I believe in, especially when I know how many people are going to see this site. I have a responsibility to those people not to let that experience be negative.

## Perfect Day

I became a designer because I like to invent, create, and innovate. Design is about looking at real-world challenges and coming up with interesting solutions that make sense, and that will delight users. I think my best days are ones when I have the opportunity to be alone and focus on the challenges I see for the next generation of the product. There are so many things I want to fix about the way we have things now, but at the same time my mind is always thinking about what we can deliver next. I work very closely with the product group, brainstorming ideas and coming up with interesting ways to do user testing. I enjoy that kind of work.

## Frustrations

For practical reasons, the team sometimes treats me as a production designer. As someone trained with visual tools, I'm often called upon to generate and update assets, frequently at the last minute. This kind of work can be tedious, but I'm the only person skilled enough to do it properly. I've seen what happens when we leave design tasks to engineers. It usually isn't pretty. The most frustrating part is when a new feature needs to be developed quickly—or may already have been built by the engineers without any design—and I have to drop everything to create layouts and assets that fit conceptually with the rest of the product. As often as not, a last-minute feature doesn't make sense conceptually from a design perspective, so this kind of work can be very draining.

## Concerns About Scrum

I try to stay on top of development techniques, and I've read some things about scrum. I've been wondering how design is supposed to be part of the scrum process, and it never seems to be very clearly spelled out. Some people say that integrating design into a scrum process is best done by carving out a separate design sprint before each development sprint, making the whole process less agile. Other approaches seem to advocate asking the designer to fit in between the cracks in the scrum process, or to become a pseudo engineering resource on the team. None of that sounds very appealing to me. I already feel as if I'm doing too much of my work at the last minute. I don't like the idea that what I do may either slow down the scrum process, or that I might find myself more time pressured by having to fit in with a scrum team.

# An Executive

## Role

I provide leadership for the entire company. That can mean a lot of different things. When it comes to engineering, it means providing direction on how the product needs to evolve based on my understanding of the marketplace. It's up to me to inspire the engineering team to create the products we need in order to stay competitive and grow.

## Motivations

Ultimately, if I don't do my job well, nobody in the company has a job. That's a big responsibility, and I take it seriously. I need to make sure the products we're developing satisfy customers and support the bottom line.

## Frustrations

Because of my perspective on the marketplace, I get a bird's-eye view of what's happening around us, and what we need to do next. I can't always tell everybody all the factors that go into the decisions I make, but I need people to trust that I know what I'm talking about when I say something needs to happen now. It's hard to build a team around you that can understand this and communicate your message to the people doing the work. It's kind of like building a ship in a bottle sometimes.

I can see what I want done, but I can't just reach in there and do it myself with my own hands.

## My Perfect Day

I have to keep track of a lot of moving parts around here. I don't have time to shepherd everybody through the process. That's why I have managers, and that's why I have to step back and let them do their jobs. As far as engineering is concerned, my perfect day is when they deliver something that I was waiting for, and that I know is going to delight our customers.

## Concerns About Scrum

I've seen a lot of initiatives come and go over the years. Every few years there's a new flavor of management system, with a new set of buzzwords that everybody's talking about. I've read a little bit about scrum, and it seems as if it might add a bit of overhead to the engineering organization. I want to keep my eye on that. Also, everything I hear seems to talk about extra meetings, and I'm sure the engineers aren't going to like that. Our engineering team is one of our most valuable resources, and I don't want to see us doing anything that might upset them.

# Summary

These perspectives only represent a subset of the possible responses you might get from your team when you try to introduce scrum. There are as many different possible issues as there are individuals, and you know the people you work with best.

The responses above show how some of the typical people you might find working on a web development project could see scrum affecting their work. Think about the motivations and frustrations of the people on your team. Do you see any of the same concerns that were raised above? Does anything they said ring true, or raise any red flags you would want to watch out for if you saw similar things happening on your team?

 **Scrum Won't Resolve Issues that Need to be Handled at the Management Level**

Happily for this team, WithKittens.com isn't dealing with individuals who are fundamentally unmotivated by the jobs they do, or unwilling to participate in the process. Those can be signals that there are deeper issues to be addressed at the management or human resources level, outside of scrum. Remember, scrum is about getting the work done and helping the team work together and improve. It's independent of the organizational hierarchy and the management process.

In the next few chapters, we're going to cover the specifics of how scrum works. We'll look in detail at the roles, rituals, and artifacts associated with the scrum process, and show how they apply to teams working in web and mobile development.

While you're reading the descriptions of scrum, keep in mind the responses above. Ask yourself whether certain organizational roles seem to map logically to any agile roles. Think about how the real people who work together on a team and in an organization might respond to the tools and techniques we'll be discussing. You may start to see how some of the frustrations and concerns raised above can be addressed by scrum.

Chapter **3**

# Scrum Roles

## Establishing Who Does What

Scrum is a system that supports sustained productivity for a team. But if you try to adopt scrum, and don't give adequate consideration to the purpose of each of the roles that scrum assigns to the participants, you're likely to find problems maintaining the balance and rhythm of scrum. Cutting corners on the defined roles is one of the most prevalent anti-patterns in scrum, and it's easily avoided by making the assignment of roles deliberate and explicit.

Traditional scrum defines only three critical roles: scrum master, product owner, and team member. We'll start with these. But scrum plays out in a context, and for web and mobile development, that context is usually a company or organization trying to create technical embodiments of experiences for clients, users, or customers.

## No Hierarchy

An agile scrum team operates within an organization that may have a hierarchy of management. But the roles in scrum are all equals as far as the process is concerned.

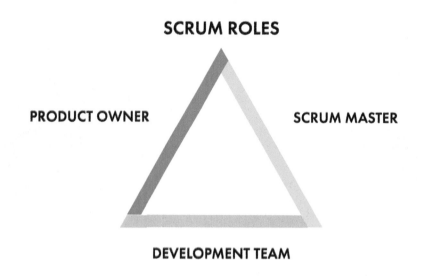

Figure 3.1. All roles are equal in scrum

Although the title may sound imposing, the scrum master has no authority other than the leadership demonstrated in the role of servant leader for the scrum process. The product owner has no authority other than maintaining the vision of the product and shepherding it through the scrum process. And the team has no authority other than the power to estimate, accept, reject, commit to, work on, and complete stories. And everyone should be empowered to enforce these roles to preserve an agile work environment.

 **A servant leader?**

The term **servant leader** is often used when discussing the delicately balanced position a scrum master occupies. The scrum master has no formal authority over anything other than the rituals and artifacts of scrum, but leads the team from within by embracing and evangelizing the concepts of scrum. A scrum master serves the needs of the entire team—helping to eliminate **blockers** (impediments to the scrum workflow) and coaching people about how to follow the practices of scrum—and should lead by example when advocating for and defending scrum.

## Scrum Roles and Organizational Roles

The roles of scrum are independent of the formal job titles that may be assigned and managed as part of the hierarchy of a company. For some teams, this can cause confusion over how the people who aren't part of the formal agile process fit into the process. Nobody outside the scrum team really needs to understand scrum for it to work. But an important part of scrum is transparency, and the activities of a scrum team may draw outside attention.

In this chapter, we'll go over the critical roles of scrum master, product owner, and team member. In addition, we'll discuss the motivations and perspectives of many people outside the scrum team whose involvement may have an effect on how well scrum works, and may ultimately be the key to advocating for and maintaining scrum in an organization.

# Scrum Master

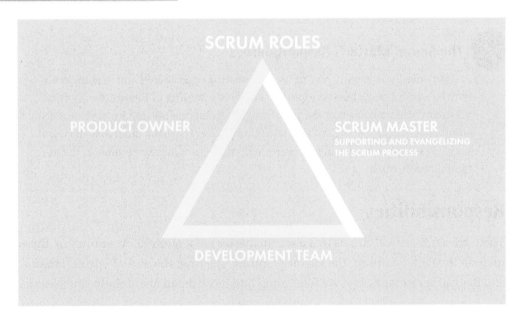

Figure 3.2. The role of the scrum master

A **scrum master** is the glue that ties a scrum team together. Scrum masters are responsible for keeping people clear on their roles, managing the rituals and artifacts of scrum (which we'll be getting to shortly), and coaching people within the team and across the organization to help overcome blockers and maintain a sustainable productive pace.

Unlike project managers, a scrum master comes with a clearly defined mission as a servant leader to the team. A scrum master has no formal authority within an organization, other than the authority to shepherd the team through the rituals of scrum, and maintain the artifacts that track the team's progress. But the scrum master has ultimate authority when it comes to the scrum process and how it's being applied.

### The Scrum Master's Involvement

The scrum master may be a part of the development team, but just as often a scrum master may have no involvement in the day-to-day development work of the team. For teams who have been following scrum practices for a while, and who are comfortable with scrum, a single scrum master with no development duties may be able to take responsibility simultaneously for two teams.

### The Scrum Master's Responsibilities

A scrum master is usually part of the Engineering department, and in some cases may be a member of the development team. It's a conflict of interest for a scrum master to be the manager of the people on a development team. A scrum master should have no formal organizational authority over the team, otherwise the team may feel inhibited about raising issues with the scrum master because of the potential ramifications.

## Responsibilities

There are a few critical rituals that a scrum master must observe. At minimum, these include the daily standup, the sprint planning meeting, the end-of-sprint demo, and the sprint retrospective. We'll be going into more detail about these rituals soon.

In addition to hosting the rituals of scrum, a scrum master is responsible for coaching the team through the scrum process. This may involve stepping boldly into discussions about individual roles and duties, and helping people communicate their needs and expectations in a way that makes them understandable. In that sense, a scrum master can become a team's advocate, counselor, and liaison to other parts of the organization.

Scrum masters also maintain a number of artifacts that help the team stay focused on their goals and measure the sustainability of their progress toward their commitments. These artifacts, and the data they contain, may be subject to broad interpretation both within the team and outside it, so a scrum master needs to be capable of explaining the state of the team and its progress in terms that are understandable to a wide range of audiences, both within and outside the organization if needed.

# A Day in the Life

Scrum masters need to be involved in every aspect of product development, so they have to work closely with many people and deal with a number of critical tools—as illustrated in the following list. (Don't worry if there are some unfamiliar terms in here at this point. We'll be discussing the artifacts and rituals of scrum soon.) So, their activities include:

- planning and hosting the rituals of scrum, including the daily standup, the sprint planning meeting, the sprint demo, and the sprint retrospective

- assisting the team in identifying blockers that get in the way of their development work

- soliciting help from team members, product owners, or anyone in the organization who can help remove blockers and get stories going again

- maintaining the artifacts of scrum and making sure everyone has access to them

- coaching team members about their roles and responsibilities, while watching for problems and helping to resolve them

- working with the product owner to help clarify stories and maintain a well-groomed backlog

- representing the needs of scrum to management and across the organization for the sake of the product and the team.

One ritual that every scrum master will try to host on a daily basis is the fifteen-minute standup with the entire team, and any guests who care to observe. For some teams, this will happen early in the day, while other teams prefer to do it later.

Scrum masters will likely be involved in a number of follow-up discussions at the end of the standup. The most important ones will involve removing blockers from team members who cannot move forward without coordinated assistance. Scrum masters will also meet with constituents such as product owners and team members to follow up on any other issues that were raised during the standup.

On days when other rituals are scheduled, such as the sprint planning meeting, the sprint demo, or the sprint retrospective, the scrum master leads the process, making sure all the steps the team has agreed to are followed, and that the time constraints are honored.

Updating the artifacts of scrum is the daily duty of the scrum master. These are always maintained in a state that allows anyone to see at a glance what the team is working on, to support the essential transparency that keeps scrum working. This includes calculating and reporting on team metrics such as velocity, and clarifying the relevance of these concepts to people outside the team.

Scrum masters also play a key role in supporting the scrum responsibilities of every member of the team. A scrum master needs to be available to coach the team when issues arise, and to recognize these issues when they manifest. This can mean helping the product owner figure out how to phrase a story for the backlog, observing and participating in a pairing session with developers to facilitate the process, or preparing reports on the team's status in plain language—for the sake of people who aren't on the team but who need to understand what's happening.

# Product Owners

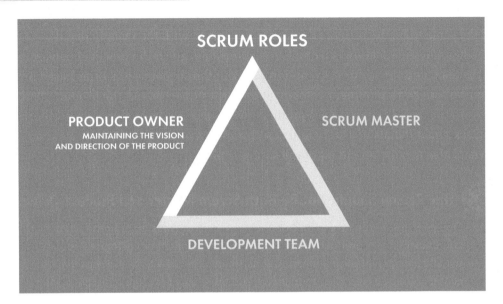

Figure 3.3. The role of the product owner

Unlike a scrum master, whose responsibilities are focused on the development team, a **product owner** has a shared responsibility to the team and to the customer. The product owner is the voice of the customer, and stands in as the representative of the customer's needs, wants, and expectations.

A product owner usually belongs to a department such as Product or Customer Support, and spends time working with customers directly to understand their needs and translate these into clear descriptions that the team can estimate and work on, using a consistent format we call stories in scrum terminology.

The product owner keeps an eye on the big picture from the customer's perspective, looking at the overall state of the product and the timeline for release cycles, and the changing technical landscape, while deciding what features are the highest priority for the team to work on in the next sprint.

Product owners work directly with designers to make sure user experience flows have been considered, and that design assets are ready for the team. They also work with QA engineers to verify that the necessary acceptance criteria are accounted for in the test suite for a story. Product owners also collaborate with the scrum master to help remove blockers from outside the team that may be getting in the way of progress.

At the same time, the product owner works closely with the team to decide whether a desired feature is technically achievable, given the practical constraints of the team and the technology, and to plan out the sequence of stories based on their historical development velocity and their feedback about the product. Being close to the team is vital, since a product owner needs to be available so developers can ask about details of a story and confirm the progress of their work. Product owners also usually attend all of the scrum rituals.

 **One Person Should Not Be Both Scrum Master and Product Owner**

One person shouldn't try to take on the roles of scrum master and product owner simultaneously. A product owner has a duty to the client or customer first, and usually isn't part of the engineering department. The objectives of a scrum master center around sustainable productivity, and these may not align with the organizational objectives of anyone reporting outside the department.

## Responsibilities

One of the most critical duties of a product owner is clarifying the needs of the customer, developing a backlog of product features to work on, and writing clear stories that communicate the full expectations for the product, while meeting the standards of the team. A well-written story needs to encapsulate the full intention for a distinct slice of functionality, including any acceptance criteria, as well as the customer's justification for needing this particular feature. Usually the product owner and the scrum master will collaborate to make sure each story is ready for the team.

Once enough stories are written to occupy the team for the upcoming sprint, a product owner keeps track of them and organizes them to make sure the sequence of development for the product is planned out efficiently and to the expectations of the customer. Meanwhile, the product owner is diligently working on stories that may be needed if the team runs out of work in the current sprint, as well as outlining and drafting items that reflect the customer's anticipated needs for sprints in the near future.

A product owner doesn't need to do detailed planning more than a sprint or two ahead of what the team may be working on. In fact, stories written too far in advance of the sprint in which they might be worked on are so frequently discarded or re-written that it's usually a waste of time to spell them out in much detail. But a good product owner maintains a vision for how the product will evolve as individual features are added, keeping in mind the importance of setting the stage in the current sprint for features that may be needed in the future.

Product owners need to be in regular communication with the customer, to make sure the stories they're writing and the backlog they're grooming meet current expectations. While scrum encourages transparency, not all teams invite customers directly into the rituals and artifacts. A product owner translates the state of the product for the customer—demonstrating and getting approval for each slice of functionality delivered—and gathers feedback from the customer to let the team know whether or not they're on the right path.

In addition, the product owner needs to be available to the team to help resolve any conflicts or clarify any details about stories the team is working on. As the internal voice of the customer, the product owner needs to embody the expectations for the product, and be able to make decisions quickly so the team can continue working.

## A Day in the Life

Product owners split their time among several responsibilities and constituents:

- meeting regularly with customers to share information about the team's progress and gather feedback about what the customer wants next

- working directly with designers to plan and prepare assets for the team

- getting technical approval from the team for stories in development

- verifying the completeness and relevance of the QA test suite

- coordinating with the scrum master to make sure everyone has the information they need to do their work

- meeting with team members when asked to clarify issues and make decisions writing stories and grooming the product backlog so it reflects the current vision for the product.

Most product owners like to attend the team's daily standup ritual. As guests, product owners are generally not permitted to ask questions or give feedback until after every member of the team has presented, unless asked directly. After the standup, product owners will often follow up on issues that were raised during the standup with the relevant parties, either on the team or outside.

While the team is working on the current sprint's stories, the product owner is constantly watching their progress. It's the product owner's prerogative to adjust the order of the stories in the current sprint if it appears that a critical slice of functionality is in danger of not being completed soon enough. The product owner may also prioritize the backlog of stories that are ready for the team to start work on if they run out of stories in the current sprint.

Product owners need to spend their days ready to answer questions about the stories that are in progress during the sprint. When a product owner can't be reached for a quick answer, the developers working on a story may be permanently blocked. For this reason, many product owners prefer to work alongside the team, so they can be available at a moment's notice.

One of the things customers love about working with agile development teams is frequent and accurate information about the state of the product. Often a product owner is in daily communication with the customer to report on progress and get insight into any issues that may be on the customer's mind.

When they aren't assisting the team or the customer, product owners are writing and refining stories for the next sprint, grooming the backlog of stories to meet the customer's vision for the product, and working with designers to make sure that everything the team will need to work on for these stories will be ready for them.

# Team Members

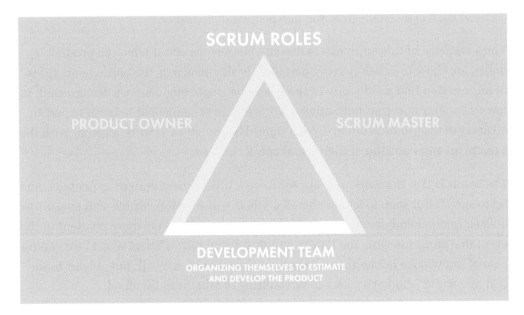

Figure 3.4. The role of the development team

Most scrum teams consist of a set of four to eight engineers. Their specializations should be planned to support the type of work the team is going to be responsible for, so they can estimate it well and produce results that meet the team's definition of done.

A team member is expected to participate actively in all the scrum rituals, and operate in a transparent way that allows everyone to be at least peripherally aware of what their teammates are working on.

## Cross-Training

Specialization is important to the development of an engineer's career, but on a scrum team it isn't assumed that any one engineer will have exclusive responsibility for any particular aspect of all stories. Part of the power of scrum is the transparency it provides, allowing engineers from all backgrounds to learn about what's involved in developing any aspect of the work the team has accepted.

Scrum encourages engineers to work together. A practice called **pair programming**, adapted from the agile technique known as Extreme Programming, is often practical for the type of work done in web and mobile projects. Pair programming advocates matching people with different levels of experience to work together on the same code, so each can benefit from the perspective of the other.

The advantage of this approach is that the knowledge about what the product is doing, and how to develop every part of it, is shared across the entire team. Silos of information that reside only in the head of a single engineer are discouraged, in favor of communication with others. Not everyone is expected to be an expert in all areas of the product, but everyone should be prepared to work together with the experts on areas outside of their usual comfort zones.

The result is that the work may appear to go a little slower at first, as people come up to speed. But soon a deeper shared context will develop, which will speed up both estimation and development. The team will also become more resilient in the event that someone wins the lottery and decides to retire. There won't be a gaping hole of knowledge left behind. There may be large shoes to fill, but at least there will be people who have some understanding of what was involved.

 **Pair Programming**

Pair programming is very demanding. Some of the expectations are that two people share a single monitor, and trade responsibility for entering code (driving) and keeping track of what needs to happen next (navigating). A pair should be talking with each other constantly as they work, and neither member of a pair should allow distractions such as email to interfere with the process. Most pairs find they can work no more than six hours a day in this mode, but the productivity gains and the benefits to the stability of the team are worth the tradeoffs.

## Responsibilities

As far as the scrum process is concerned, a team member is responsible for the quality of the product being developed, and for the preservation of the scrum process for the entire team. These are two aspects that every team member has the authority to affect by the way they perform their duties.

The quality of the product is supported by the team's ability to accept or reject stories. If stories are presented that aren't fully clear, or that may be impossible or impractical given the history of the project, the team should put the quality of their work first and insist that the product owner rewrite or retract the stories.

Estimating the effort involved in doing the work to complete a story is also part of the team's responsibilities. As a team works together and gains experience with different stories, they should begin to develop a shared and subjective scale of relative effort involved in stories of a similar nature. The effort, usually measured in arbitrary points, is assigned by the team to help establish how much work they can do within a timeframe. That helps the product owner plan how quickly new features can be completed.

The team is expected to push back against any attempts to sacrifice quality for the sake of speed, given the practical constraints of the project. Additionally, the team should be tracking the overall quality of the codebase, and proposing stories that would refactor the existing code to enhance maintainability, or to support emerging technical standards. Keeping the code clean, self-documenting, and internally consistent helps everyone on the team work together more effectively.

Every member of the team is also responsible for maintaining the scrum process for every other member. If anyone interrupts the standup, or tries to introduce changes to a story in the middle of a sprint, every team member should feel authorized to interrupt that behavior. Anyone on the team should have the authority to point out when scrum is being sidestepped.

It's critical for team members to take this responsibility for their fellow team members seriously. The power of scrum is in the dynamic it creates among a group of people. Failing to defend the scrum process is letting the other team members down.

 ## All Team Member Are Equal

Although the members of a team may report to one or more managers inside or outside of the scrum context, within a scrum team all team members are considered equals. The team members shouldn't report to the product owner or to the scrum master because that creates a tension between the agile roles and every employee's independent place in an organization's hierarchy. If seniority or reporting relationships exist among employees within the scrum team, they should be ignored when it comes to following the scrum process. Anyone who notices organizational rank being used to influence the scrum process should bring the matter to the attention of the scrum master, either at the time, during a retrospective, or confidentially.

# A Day in the Life

Most days, a team member will be working on code for the majority of the day, in blocks of time as long and as constant as can be arranged. A team member's core daily duties are fairly straightforward:

- developing, checking, testing, and documenting code
- getting clarifications, story details, and feedback from the product owner
- participating in the rituals of scrum
- working with the scrum master to remove blockers for fellow team members.

The most prevalent image that springs to mind when picturing a scrum team is probably the team's participation in a daily standup ritual, which we'll be discussing in more detail in the chapter on scrum rituals. Every team member is expected to be available and prepared for this brief, fifteen-minute window of time. A team will usually try to schedule this so that it won't interfere with the flow of work for the team.

### When to Do the Standup

For some teams, scheduling the standup right before or after lunch, or at the beginning of the work day, makes the most sense. Teams that are not co-located may need to choose a time that works for people across multiple time zones. The time can always be adjusted by the team in response to feedback gathered during sprint retrospectives.

On days when other scrum rituals are scheduled, all team members are expected to be present and participate actively. The rituals of scrum are designed to make efficient use of limited time, while producing predictable and valuable results. A good scrum master will arrange to maintain a time box around each ritual so the time commitment and the end result are predictable.

Other than participating in the rituals of scrum, all team members should be spending their days taking stories from ready to done. If the organization interferes with this work by creating excessive meetings, the team should bring this issue to the scrum master so that it can be addressed. Preserving the uninterrupted time a developer needs to concentrate on coding is one of scrum's top priorities.

# Team Resources

A scrum team doesn't work in a vacuum. There's usually an organization that exists around scrum, and that supports the efforts of the scrum team with the resources it needs to produce the work. There's a two-way relationship that must be maintained between the scrum team and the rest of the organization, so that each is able to benefit from the process.

Just as the organization and its hierarchy should have no influence on the rituals, artifacts, and roles of scrum, scrum has no formal opinions about how the outer organization is structured. Scrum can exist successfully in a rigidly tiered company with clearly defined titles and roles just as easily as it can work in a "holacracy" (an organization without any formal chain of command). As long as the scrum team is provided with the resources it needs, and can justify its existence by producing the results that the organization wants, the relationship should be maintainable.

There are sometimes different opinions about how the resources a team needs should be provided. An agile approach to working this out is to try one way, notice how well it works, and iterate to find what's most productive.

In particular, there are a few key resources most scrum teams doing web and mobile development find themselves needing that aren't formally defined as part of scrum.

## Designers

A critical input into any web or mobile project is design. Designers help establish the user experience, the flow, and the visual consistency of a project. With the trend toward design thinking as a process, designers have become elemental in all phases of product development, from initial problem definition through wireframing, creating style guides, building graphical assets, validating visual consistency, and doing user experience testing.

Designers work closely with product owners during the development of new stories. In most cases design choices drive ideation, and much of the innovation in how a product evolves iteratively comes from the designer. But designers also need to be available to team members when questions of layout and style come up. Sometimes designers need to be prepared to drop everything and produce assets, or make decisions that are critical to unblock developers in the middle of a story. Switching between high-concept thinking and detailed, hands-on production can make the designer's role very challenging.

Some teams choose to integrate designers into the team, and include them in all the rituals. The advantage of this approach is that the designer is constantly aware of how the team is working, and able to give immediate feedback by participating during story creation as well as estimation and development. A designer who chooses to work as part of the team should be prepared to commit to the scrum process just like any other team member.

However, unlike most members of a scrum team, a designer is usually not trained or inclined to work as an engineer, or to pair with other engineers on development work. Additionally, the skills and responsibilities of a designer may not lend themselves to paired work with engineers not trained in design themselves. Because of this, a designer who's integrated into the team may need to be treated differently from other team resources. This can sometimes create a sense of imbalance, leaving the design role feeling poorly integrated.

Another approach that many teams use is to create an extended sprint sequence, with a separate design sprint that precedes the development sprint. This helps isolate the work of designers from the work of engineers, while still keeping designers integrated into the scrum process as members of the team.

Using the design sprint approach can be effective, but it limits the agility of scrum. Because design sprints happen before development sprints, the team is effectively committing to working in increments that are twice as long. This means that the product owner's ability to adjust requirements needs to be pushed out an additional sprint, so changes need to be planned that much further in advance. For some teams this may be a good solution, as long as they're prepared to accept the tradeoffs.

A third method worth considering is maintaining a separate Design team, and treating them as a resource. Designers on the Design team can be called upon to participate in the ideation, story creation, asset development, user flow testing, or anything that the scrum process needs. Because the designers are independent of the scrum process, they're welcome to attend the rituals as guests, but aren't required to be active participants.

A Design team that operates as an independent resource may choose to structure itself using a different agile approach known as **kanban**. Kanban is similar to scrum, but instead of operating in sprints with contracted deliverables at predetermined intervals, a kanban team commits to a specified amount of work-in-progress. Kanban teams can accept new stories from the product owner without advance planning, as long as the resources of the team are never committed to more than the amount of work they're capable of doing sustainably.

 **Kanban**

The details of kanban are more complex than what we've covered here, but it's another approach worth looking into for organizing work that involves a constant flow of services. In particular, kanban is very effective for managing the workflow of organizations such as Operations and Customer Support, where there's a steady stream of similar stories that all need to be addressed, and that frequently require rapid response on a priority basis.

# QA Engineers

Quality assurance is the responsibility of every member of the team, but most organizations have professionals who are specially trained in the techniques of creating and managing test suites. For web and mobile work, this can be an intricate and complex process, involving tools that simulate the behavior of a wide range of devices and browsers, and automation to follow both common and uncommon paths through a product.

QA engineers may be isolated into their own group, working independently of the team doing the development of the product. When this is the case, coordination with the team is critical. Unless QA is taken into account early, a scrum team may find itself rushing to complete stories before the sprint demo meeting, and then dumping a load of work onto the QA team at the last minute, so that stories will be ready to demo.

Not unlike designers, QA engineers are sometimes given a separate sprint to do their testing. This avoids the issue of trying to get the stories verified quickly at the end of every sprint, but it introduces the same kind of reduced flexibility as having a separate design sprint. Further, when it comes time for a demo of the stories, most of the team has already moved on to newer stories, and the details of the previous sprint's work may not be fresh in their minds.

The biggest problem with isolating QA from development is that engineers feel free to take on the next story on their list before the previous story has been verified as done. Frequently in a web and mobile context, stories will build on each other in subtle ways, even if the stories are technically independent. This can lead to situations where the work on a new story needs to be redone based on inconsistencies found when testing a prior story.

Ideally, QA should be considered part of the team's definition of "done" for any story. This means that QA engineers should start writing the tests for a story at the same time that developers are creating the code. The QA cycle for a story should be part of the sprint, and the developers working on a story shouldn't abandon it to start something new until QA has been completed.

On some teams, QA engineers are integrated into the team directly. This provides a number of advantages. The skills and training of development and QA engineers are complementary, and people in both roles can benefit professionally from pairing with each other to learn more about the techniques and approaches they use. A team with integrated QA engineers also naturally considers testing and validation as part of the effort of rendering a story done, and makes sure stories are sized and scheduled appropriately to include that.

## Operations

The folks who keep the networks running and handle technical support for a company are often part of the same Engineering department that's the home of the product development team. Because of this, some companies try to integrate the people on these teams into their scrum process. But the structure of the organization shouldn't influence the needs of a scrum team.

Unless there is a compelling reason, it can be a bad practice to try to integrate Operations engineers into a product development scrum team. While the people in Operations are trained engineers, the responsibilities they handle should live independent of the product development process. Keeping the networks up, the computers running, and the servers online is constant and challenging in a different way than product development. It can be dangerous to confuse these roles[1].

---

[1] Not unlike design or customer service, it can be practical to treat Operations as a separate team, perhaps using a kanban approach to help them manage their sustainable workflow and prioritization.

It's always important to keep Operations informed as product development progresses, so that any changes in the product that might have an impact on the reliable availability of services and resources can be considered. A good scrum team includes engineers and product owners who can recognize when changes may have an impact on system or network load, and will call in the opinions of qualified Operations engineers to help with planning for a story.

 **Operations and Pair Programming**

It may be impractical to pull Operations professionals away from their duties to pair on development, although it can be useful for developers to pair occasionally with Operations engineers to enhance their understanding of the issues that affect the availability of the product.

# Managers

One of the benefits of scrum is that teams have the opportunity to self organize and figure out the best way to develop the product iteratively, testing things out, making changes, and improving as they go. What this means is that the team takes responsibility for what they do, and organizes themselves around the goal of completing the work in the most efficient way possible. As a result, sometimes managers can be confused about their role in a scrum organization.

The self-organizing nature of scrum doesn't have anything to do with the hierarchy of the company that assigns a manager in a different role and a set of responsibilities relative to an employee. Scrum should have no opinion about the hierarchy of the organization, just as the hierarchy of the organization should have no impact on the scrum process.

In any company, management is a vital role. Managers are responsible for hiring, firing, allocating resources, and representing the employees throughout the organization. Without managers, employees would have nobody to turn to in the event that there's a problem outside the scrum process that needs to be addressed. Managers often have responsibility for the productivity of the team, including reporting results to senior executives, and demonstrating the value of the scrum process as it's working.

Managers may also participate as developers on a scrum team. Often people in management roles in engineering also have deeper experience with some of the problems the team may be facing. These managers may serve as architects or senior developers, and may have valuable knowledge to share. Within the scrum team, a manager is treated as one of the developers, and given no other authority than any developer on the team.

### Managers as Developers

In some organizations, the role of manager is viewed with disdain. We've all seen the image of the pointy haired boss from Dilbert cartoons. One of the advantages of scrum is that it doesn't care how the manager performs outside of the scrum process, as long as sufficient resources are provided to support a continuing scrum process. An effective scrum team should operate independent of these preconceptions, but the opportunity to work with a manager as a peer on a scrum team can help improve communications outside scrum as well.

Employees on the team who feel uncomfortable about interacting with their manager as a peer, or managers who feel uncomfortable with their reduced authority within scrum, should discuss the issue with the scrum master. A strong scrum master will be experienced in dealing with issues around management and authority, and how it relates to scrum.

# The Rest of the World

A scrum team doesn't operate in a vacuum. Outside the scrum team, there's an organization that needs a product developed, for whatever reason. Part of the responsibilities of the scrum master is to evangelize the value of scrum to the rest of the company. Along with that comes the responsibility to make sure scrum actually is serving the needs of the company and the constituents of the scrum process.

Among these constituents are senior executives within the company, users of the product being developed, customers who may have commissioned the creation of the product—whether inside the company or outside—and other groups inside the company.

From the outside, scrum can seem like a mystery. Despite the emphasis on transparency, the terminology of scrum can confuse people who aren't familiar with what the terms actually mean. The artifacts and charts that scrum creates may seem to imply meaning that just isn't there. Any confusion from outside the scrum team can influence the stability of scrum, both in terms of resources being allocated, and the flow of stories into the process.

## Users

One of the most obvious constituents of the scrum team is the set of users the product is being developed to support. The user should be visible in practically every story, even if the story doesn't affect the front-end interface of the website, or show up on the screen of the mobile device. Administrative users are users. Content managers who populate the product are users. Anyone who interacts with the product is a user.

To the user, the fact that the product was developed with the scrum process is irrelevant. However, user testing is an important part of iterative development. Much of scrum happens in organizations that are using lean development practices. This means starting with a minimum viable product, and then iterating as the user experience testing indicates.

Instrumentation to make sure that user experience can be captured and tracked effectively is usually important for web and mobile products developed with a scrum approach. Without instrumentation to track clicks, gestures, goals, and interactions with critical features, the product owner will have fewer data points for reference when it comes time to decide what stories are most important to work on next. The intent of scrum is to support an agile process that allows quick adjustments in product direction based on real user needs.

## Customers

The customer for a product being developed with scrum may be a client of the company, or may be an internal department inside the company. Regardless, direct interaction with the customer is the responsibility of the product owner. A strong product owner will shield the team from the customer, and protect the customer from feeling disconnected.

Customers may or may not know what they want. Often a customer will have an idea, and it'll need to be worked out through the scrum process. This may mean several rounds of work with designers, and perhaps a few iterations through the product development process. As a result, the desired path from vision to reality may not be as straight as a customer may wish. Product owners step in, keeping the customer informed and satisfied, while clarifying the customer's vision to the point that a team can estimate it and work on it productively.

A good product owner is a strong line of defense between the team and the chaos of direct interaction with the customer. This isn't an easy role to fill, since the customer is either paying the bills, or working for another department inside the same company. The support of a strong scrum master may be needed to help defend the scrum team. If the team feels they're getting too much direct influence from the customer—that isn't properly filtered through the product owner—they should feel free to engage the scrum master to help improve the process.

## Executives and Other Employees

A scrum master is both a coach and an evangelist when it comes to the rest of the company. Scrum masters need to be able to represent the power and value of scrum effectively, and explain it in terms that don't rely on the custom vocabulary of scrum. Not only will the process attract interest from other employees, but also from executives, who will rightly be concerned about the value provided.

Happily, scrum generates a lot of data. Among the artifacts of scrum will be real-world information about how much work the team can do in a given amount of time, how many stories have been completed, what features have been produced, working software to demonstrate, and the feedback of the team, the product owners, and the customers. The scrum master may choose to formulate reports for different audiences, host brown-bag lunches to explain scrum, or invite people to attend scrum rituals to see for themselves what's going on.

While managers are responsible for securing the resources necessary to support their employees, a scrum master is responsible for getting the buy-in and organizational support for the scrum process. If scrum is running well, everyone on the team will be an evangelist for it. Encourage scrum participants to let other employees know how it's working. Positive word-of-mouth around the company is good for the careers of everyone on the scrum team, as well as the stability of the scrum process.

# Summary

The roles of scrum have been clearly defined so that there is a balance of power among equals, and all of the responsibilities of developing a product in an agile manner are handled.

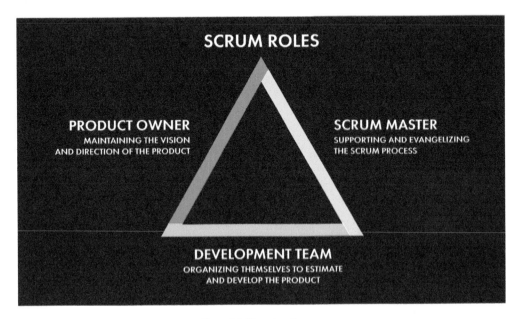

Figure 3.5. The roles of scrum

▦ A scrum master hosts the rituals of scrum, supports the team, and evangelizes the scrum process, both inside and outside of scrum.

▦ A product owner maintains the vision and direction of the product, and is responsible for interacting with the customer.

▦ A development team is made up of engineers who organize themselves to estimate and do the work to build the product.

Now that we've gone over the roles involved in scrum, in the next chapter we'll take a look at the rituals they engage in. Watch and see how the people in these roles can interact to support their agendas, and how the sturdy balance they achieve helps keep scrum teams productive.

# 4

## Scrum Rituals

The practice of working on a scrum team is organized into a series of rituals. The rituals mark key events in the process of carrying out the work of a sprint. It's the responsibility of the scrum master to host each of the rituals, and make sure that they focus on their objectives, and produce the desired results for the benefit of the entire team.

## What Are Rituals?

Each **ritual** is a face-to-face gathering in real time, which takes people away from the work they're doing, and offers them the opportunity to have targeted communication with each other about the context of that work. Scrum favors communication over documentation, which is why it provides regular and clearly defined opportunities for various types of useful face-to-face communication.

## Not Another Meeting!

Many people who work in companies are allergic to meetings, and for good reason. They may have been overwhelmed by too many meetings, taking up too much of their time, and not producing any results. They may be used to having meetings called to address every little issue, without any one person being responsible for making sure the issue gets resolved. Meetings can take people away from the work they're doing, and interrupt their focus, often without providing much value in return.

Let's face it, most companies are *terrible* at meetings.

Unlike the usual meeting, every ritual in scrum has a specific objective, addresses a particular audience, has a defined time frame within which to accomplish its goals, and has a predictable set of outcomes. Everyone attending a ritual knows before the ritual starts what to expect, how to behave, and what the result of the commitment is supposed to be. The rituals of scrum are mindful of their overall purpose, and respect the time and attention of the participants.

## Time Boxing

One of the most important concepts in scrum rituals is that of the **time box**. It's the responsibility of the scrum master who hosts the rituals to keep everybody aware of exactly how long they have committed for this ritual, and how far along they are at any point within it.

Often scrum masters will write the time up on the whiteboard in front of the room, or keep a large clock visible so everybody can keep track of the time. (I have been known to bring a small cube-shaped clock labeled "Time Box" to rituals, and display it where everyone can see it.) The concept of time boxing empowers all the active participants in a ritual to encourage each other to get to the point when necessary, and remain focused on the objectives of the ritual.

 **How long should each time box be?**

The length of time the team will spend on each ritual usually depends on the number of weeks allocated per sprint. The only ritual that must stay within a 15 minute time box is the daily standup. Teams come to an agreement on the time box for each ritual as part of the process of iterating and improving how they organize themselves for scrum. I've provided a few suggestions below for teams to start with.

Scrum shows its respect for the time and commitment of every participant by establishing at the beginning of each ritual what the time box is, and how that time will be allocated for the different aspects of the ritual. All participants are expected to remain engaged and participate during the time box of the ritual, with the promise that the ritual won't be extended without a good and practical reason, and not unless all participants agree to the extension.

If a ritual appears to be about to exceed its time box, the scrum master should ask everybody for their permission to continue the ritual for a specific length of time. That way everybody knows up front how much time to budget, and everybody has to agree if the budget needs to be extended.

Of course, we are all human, and side issues will come up during rituals that feel as if they need to be discussed right then and there. Keeping the focus on the ritual at hand is the responsibility of the scrum master, as well as the rest of the team. A good scrum master needs to keep track of these issues, and maintain respect for the time box of the ritual in progress for the sake of everyone involved.

Making sure that important side discussions don't get lost is a shared responsibility, but the scrum master needs to be prepared to take an active role in that process. People will more willingly set aside an off-topic discussion if confident that they'll be able to pick it up again later.

## The Length of the Sprint

Teams have some choices to make when it comes to choosing the length of the sprint. Sprint length should allow the types of stories the team expects to work on to be completed, according to the team's own definition of done, within a single sprint. For many teams, a short sprint of just one week matches well with short stories that are easy to finish in a week. Some teams prefer to work with more complex stories that couldn't be completed within a one week sprint, so they opt for two-week, three-week, or even four-week or longer sprints.

The length of the sprint is another factor that can be modified based on feedback received from the team, but it's important for a team to choose a length and stick with it for several sprints. Otherwise, the team may never benefit from the regularity so they can learn how to size stories consistently and estimate them correctly from one sprint to the next. Often the option to change sprint length can be addressed just by improving the way stories are written, so they can be completed within a sprint.

**Two Weeks is a Good Starting Point**

For web and mobile teams, a two-week sprint is a good place to start. Two weeks is long enough to complete most stories that relate to web and mobile projects, including the release process in most cases. If your web or mobile team is just starting out with scrum, it's worth trying a two-week sprint cycle first, to see how well it suits you.

Even if your stories tend to be short and finite, there are disadvantages to one-week sprints that are worth considering. Some of the longer rituals are repeated once every sprint. Having a one-week sprint means that repeating these rituals so frequently may start to get in the way of productivity. Some rituals, such as the retrospective, could even end up being short-changed or bypassed some weeks, and that can lead to a breakdown in the iterative improvement aspect of scrum.

A team that tends to produce more complex stories may prefer longer sprints. Keep in mind that sprints longer than two weeks mean that issues will take longer to surface, and adjustments to the backlog will need to be delayed until a sprint has been completed. Longer sprints also encourage the creation of more complex stories. The goal of scrum for web and mobile teams should be to create stories that are simple and distinct.

Figure 4.1. Two-week Sprint Cycle

This diagram represents a two-week cycle for a typical web or mobile development sprint. Each smaller circle represents a single workday, and the rituals are marked out assuming that the sprint starts at the top and loops around every two weeks.

In the next few pages, we're going to do a deep dive into each of these rituals, making sure you understand how they work, and how they can be applied to web and mobile development.

# Sprint Planning

The ritual that marks the beginning of each sprint is called sprint planning. Sprint planning is hosted by the scrum master, but the person responsible for most of the content that goes into a sprint planning is the product owner.

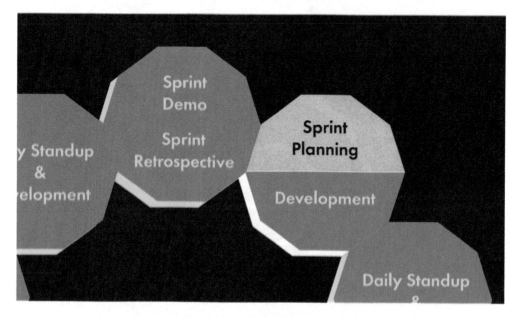

Figure 4.2. Sprint Planning

## Objective

The purpose of the sprint planning is to set the agenda for the upcoming sprint. The team gets together with the product owner and the scrum master to get an introduction to the stories that should be completed during the next sprint.

The product owner shows how the stories fit into the vision for the product, and the team estimates the stories the product owner has introduced and commits to completing as many as they believe they're capable of, given their historical velocity—which is determined by the number of points they've been able to complete in an average sprint. At the end of the sprint planning there should be a commitment to a certain set of stories that everyone can agree on. The stories should all be clear, and the amount of work they represent should be within the capacity of the team to complete during the next sprint.

# Time Box

Depending on the number of weeks a team has committed to for each sprint, the sprint planning may take several hours, or it may take an entire day. For a two-week sprint, a team may find that setting aside three or four hours is a good investment for a sprint planning. That might seem like a lot of time, but sprint planning done right is very detailed and explicit about what the team needs to produce. A key value of scrum is the communication it facilitates. Sprint planning exemplifies this.

Most teams will find they're able to accomplish the objectives of these rituals more efficiently as they get more familiar with the process. Having a strong scrum master who maintains a clear time box around the different aspects of the ritual can help make the process go as smoothly as possible.

But there's a lot to get done during the sprint planning, and these rituals need to be given adequate room to accommodate all the issues that will come to the surface. Starting with clear time constraints gives everyone confidence that there's a goal and an end point in mind, and also helps keep people focused.

## Preparation

In preparation for this ritual, the product owner will have been working with designers, customers, various team members, and the scrum master to create a backlog of clear and specific stories that have the highest priority for the product.

It's the responsibility of the product owner to make sure each of these stories is ready to be worked on, and phrased in such a way that any team member can read and understand each story's description and acceptance criteria.

# Introducing New Stories

Sprint planning provides the opportunity for the scrum team to get an introduction to the stories the product owner wants them to work on for the next iteration of the product. During this part of the ritual, the product owner goes over the stories that have been prepared, presenting them to the team for evaluation.

It's important for every member of the team to participate actively during this presentation, because this is their opportunity to question and challenge the completeness and appropriateness of each story. A good product owner will have discussed the stories with experts on the team before this ritual, to make sure that predictable objections have been addressed.

Sprint planning encourages active discussion around each story. The process opens up a dialogue, allowing the product owner and the team to consider the ramifications and feasibility of each story in detail. Although the product owner is authorized to set the priority of the stories on the sprint backlog, the team has the authority to reject stories that it considers impossible, inadequately defined, or technically inappropriate before they're added to the sprint backlog.

This part of the sprint planning ritual is also when the team has the responsibility to present stories that relate to the code itself. If the product owner is responsible for the vision of the product, the development team is responsible for the quality and maintainability of the code. The product-oriented focus of scrum is not an excuse to ignore technical debt.

Often the team will introduce stories around refactoring code, updating code to meet new standards, or making crucial upgrades to the infrastructure. It's important for the team to make a strong case, because the product owner has ultimate authority. Different teams resolve this balance of power in different ways, and it's up to each team to figure out how best to address technical debt while still meeting the expectations of product development.

## Story Estimation

The next phase of sprint planning is **story estimation**. During this process, the team will estimate the relative level of effort required to accomplish each story, based on the team's experience with similar stories in the past and their agreed definition of done.

There are many ways that teams estimate stories. The important thing to keep in mind when estimating is that the values assigned to the different stories are arbitrary and relative, and bear no resemblance to actual time. The point of the estimating exercise is to improve the team's ability to look at a new story and figure out how much effort it'll take relative to other stories they've already worked on.

Most teams use a system of **points** to estimate stories. A smaller, easy story may be estimated at one point, while a large or complex story may be assigned 20 points. Many teams use a modified Fibonacci scale, with the numbers 0, 1, 2, 3, 5, 8, 13, and 20 representing increasing levels of effort. The goal over time is for the team to get a sense of how many points they can accomplish within the single sprint, so they can estimate forward more effectively.

Each team comes up with its own sense of what every point value means for itself. There can be no logical comparison between the points accomplished by one team during the sprint and the points accomplished by a different team during the same sprint. The value of the points is subjective, and relevant only to the participants of a specific team.

Other systems for sizing stories include T-shirt sizing—such as small, medium, large, extra-large. It's completely up to the team what system they choose. Once the team has chosen a system, they should try to stick with it for several sprints, so that they can start to get a sense, over time, of what their velocity is in the metric they've chosen.

 **Everyone Should Agree**

It's important for everybody on the team to agree to the point estimate for a story, regardless of whether every member of the team will be working on that particular story. This is part of the transparency of scrum. Everyone on the team should be able to understand every story well enough to estimate its relative level of effort, and when one team member is working on a story, everyone should have at least a concept of what that story is.

## Bugs

Other stories that are usually not assigned points are bugs. A **bug** has a specific definition in scrum, and it has nothing to do with unexpected or unwanted behavior in an existing product. Bugs in scrum are missed requirements for stories that are still in progress, or that have already been accepted as done in a prior sprint.

If the team has completed a story, and it was accepted, and the points were included in the total for a sprint, but it later turns out the story was not completed correctly, no points are assigned for fixing the bugs to bring the story to a done state.

Bug work does take away from the team's velocity, because it addresses points that were included in the velocity calculation inappropriately. That should be true regardless of whether the bug is fixed in the same sprint or in a subsequent sprint.

As long as the team received points for a story that didn't meet the acceptance criteria, the work to get it to the true done state shouldn't count toward the points in any sprint.

 **You Don't Need to Set Aside Capacity for Bugs**

It's not necessary to set aside a percentage of the team's capacity to deal with bugs. The amount of work the team can predictably complete in a typical sprint includes the effort applied to fixing bugs when stories were accepted as done, but didn't actually meet all the acceptance criteria.

## Tasks

There's an old joke that scrum is a system for improving a team's ability to ship technical debt. Certainly there's more to developing a web or mobile application than just tacking on a bunch of features onto an ever-growing, increasingly complex code base. Eventually that code needs to be re-factored, infrastructure changes will have to be worked on, and a team won't be able to do effective work on new features until these issues are addressed. These necessary improvements may have no specific value for the customer, but they are necessary to keep the code from becoming stale or difficult to maintain.

Tasks relating to code maintenance should be included in the work done by the team, and prioritized in the sprint backlog, but should not be estimated with points. The points in scrum measure the ability of the team to deliver value to the customer, and are related to feature development. They are not a measure of the overall amount of work the team is doing.

A task usually does not deliver any tangible user value. But tasks need to be done, and a negotiation needs to happen between the team and the product owner during the sprint planning if the team recognizes that necessary work to keep systems maintainable and avoid technical debt is being deferred in favor of new features.

## Spikes

Most of the stories that make it to a sprint planning should be within the technical capability of the team, but occasionally there will be stories that require deeper research. Such stories trigger new tasks called **spikes**. Spikes are usually not assigned points. However, a proper spike does have acceptance criteria. There should be a clear and agreed outcome for any spike.

Spikes take away from the resources of the team, while individuals go and research technical solutions that may be beyond the team's current capabilities. As a result, the more spikes that are required to accomplish the goals of the product owner, the lower the number of points the team can accomplish in a sprint.

Due to the unknown nature of spikes, they can eat up a lot of a team's resources unless they're constrained. Generally, when agreeing to include a spike in a sprint, the team will decide on a maximum amount of time and effort that can be committed before the spike must be concluded or abandoned.

## Committing to a Sprint Backlog

Once all the stories that the product owner has presented have been estimated, all the participants in the ritual work together to come up with a backlog that makes sense for the upcoming sprint. This backlog will be sized based on the historical number of points that the team has been able to accomplish in the past, balanced against the point estimates for the new stories.

While the product owner has final authority over the contents of the sprint backlog, as well as the order of the sprint backlog, the team has the opportunity to advocate for certain changes while the backlog is being prepared.

For example, although each story should stand alone, it may make sense to the team to work on particular stories in a certain order. The team may also wish to complete stories that were started but not finished in the previous sprint. Completing stories that are in progress is useful for the development team because it helps them to maintain continuity. While there's a cost to loss of continuity, that cost is the responsibility of the product owner, and the product owner has the authority to make those decisions for the sake of the product.

Once a final sprint backlog has been created, everyone on the team needs to commit to that backlog. This is the last opportunity for the team to object, or raise issues that they think may have an impact on their ability to do the work required. If there's still disagreement, the scrum master needs to step in and facilitate the conversation so that agreement can be reached.

The end product of a sprint planning is a sprint backlog that everyone on the team can agree to. The scrum master should poll the room to make sure everyone agrees that the commitment is realistic, and that they are willing to take it on for the upcoming sprint. Then the new stories should be entered in order of priority into the tracking tools the team has agreed to use for the sprint backlog.

Sprint planning reminds everybody exactly where they are in the process of building the product owner's vision for the product, and what the objectives are for the upcoming increment. At the end of sprint planning, everyone on the team should have a good sense of what they need to do next, and a firm commitment to a set of prioritized stories to complete over the duration of the upcoming sprint.

# Daily Standup

The daily standup is probably the first ritual that comes to mind when people think of scrum. The daily standup provides a heartbeat for the team, giving everybody a regular opportunity to get a clear picture of what other people on the team are working on, and what the status of the project as a whole is.

Figure 4.3. Daily Standup

# Objective

The purpose of the daily standup is to give everybody on the team an opportunity to share the status of the work they're doing, and get help if anything is blocking their progress. Everyone on the team should pay attention as their teammates report, so they can have a clear picture of the status of the complete iteration they're all working on.

This is also an opportunity for anybody outside the team who's interested in knowing what the team is working on to find out how stories are progressing, and what's likely to be worked on next. Only team members are allowed to present at the daily standup, but anybody in the company may attend, and visitors should be invited to participate as silent observers.

# Time Box

Traditionally, the daily standup is limited to 15 minutes. It's a short ritual, and it's kept short and made as convenient as possible so that everyone can commit to being present, participating actively, and paying attention while other people are speaking. Everyone is expected to stand, both so that they pay attention, and to encourage all participants to play their part in keeping the ritual short and focused. Most teams try to hold the standup away from their desks, and discourage people from using laptops and other devices during the ritual.

 **Keeping the Standup to Time**

Keeping the daily standup within its 15 minute time box is the responsibility of the scrum master, but everybody on the team should feel empowered to enforce the rules of the standup, so the time box doesn't get broken. That includes making sure everybody starts on time, pays attention, and doesn't allow interruptions from guests.

Different teams will choose different times of day to hold the stand up. Often first thing in the morning, or right before lunch, can be good times. These are natural breaks in the day that are usually common to most people on the team, so a 15 minute standup won't disrupt the focus needed for longer blocks of programming time.

Finding a time that works for everybody can be challenging for teams that aren't co-located, especially when some members of the team are in different time zones. Nobody should be allowed to miss the standup on a regular basis, but there's always room for flexibility, as long as the objectives of the daily standup are being met. Even if not everybody can make it to a specific standup, the scrum master should keep the ritual for anyone who is there.

Sometimes teams may need to come up with their own systems, and iterate on these reflectively from sprint to sprint. The priority should be on keeping the rituals brief, maintaining them reliably, and making sure they provide the intended value without creating undue interruption.

## Preparation

Every team member should be present and available at the time of the standup. The only preparation necessary is for each team member to think about how to present the work being done at the moment in such a way that it'll be clear and understandable to everybody. if a team member is having blockers that relate to people outside the team, it's reasonable to let those people know to be prepared to discuss the issue immediately after the standup.

There's no special preparation needed by the scrum master before the standup. A good scrum master may check the status of the stories being worked on before the standup, to see if any changes are pending, or may arrange to round up any guests the scrum master thinks should be there who don't normally attend.

## Three Questions

The core of the daily standup consists of the scrum master going around the team and asking every person three questions:

- What have you done since the last stand up?
- What do you plan to do until the next standup?
- Is there anything blocking your progress?

It should be as simple as that. Every member of the team answers each one of these questions, and once the last person has finished reporting, the standup is over. Unless the scrum master has urgent announcements that need to be made for the entire team, everyone who doesn't have specific business with another person attending the standup should be free to get back to work.

 ## Beware Guests at Standups

There's a strong tendency for people attending standups as guests to ask questions, introduce new information, or start discussions that don't relate to the entire team. Anyone who isn't a member of the development team shouldn't be speaking during standup. The scrum master needs to be strong about suppressing this kind of behavior. People of high rank in the organizational hierarchy don't get special treatment in this regard. Everyone needs to respect the time and attention of the engineers, and allow them to get back to work as quickly as possible.

In answering the questions of the standup, each engineer needs to be prepared with a succinct description of what they've worked on, what they plan to work on next, and whether they have any blockers. This is a skill that takes practice, and the scrum master should be prepared to coach every team member on how to answer these questions in a way that makes the best use of the time available.

If one person's report invites a little bit of back-and-forth discussion, and the conversation has relevance for the entire team, the scrum master may permit it. But this type of interaction must be limited to respect the time box of the standup. If the conversation gets beyond a few sentences, the scrum master should step in and suggest that the conversation be taken off-line. A good scrum master will keep track of what conversations need to happen at the end of the standup, and follow up on their status afterward.

## Other Status Updates

Some teams choose to update the status of their stories on the team's shared scrum board during the daily standup, while others prefer to do it individually as the stories get completed. In either case, the standup should be an opportunity to make sure everybody has updated the status of everything they're working on, and that everybody on the team is aware of what everybody else is working on.

For teams that are doing pair programming, the standup can be an opportunity to switch pairs, or switch stories. Some teams that do pairing prefer that every story have one engineer seeing it through from beginning to end. It can be beneficial for the flexibility of the team to allow multiple people to pair on the same story, particularly if it relates to some core functionality that's worth sharing information about. Different teams will come up with different approaches, but the standup is a good place to make changes on a daily basis.

Standups are also a good opportunity for team members to let each other know if they expect to complete a story before the next standup, and if they have vacation time coming up. Knowing the availability of other people on the team can inspire teammates to plan their work around upcoming stories, and arrange to switch pairs or allocate resources appropriately.

 **What to work on next?**

If an engineer is unclear about what should be worked on next, the priority of the sprint backlog should guide these decisions. The product owner is responsible for grooming the sprint backlog throughout the sprint, and making sure that it always represents the priority in which the stories should be addressed.

Unless there's a compelling technical reason, any engineer without a current story should start working on the story at the top of the backlog with the next highest priority, regardless of specialization. Following this pattern can provide an opportunity for engineers to pair with somebody in an area where they have less experience, and help spread knowledge about the entire code base throughout the team.

Finally, the scrum master may make announcements that have relevance to the entire team at the end of the standup—once everybody has had a chance to report, and only if there's time left. This shouldn't become a replacement for any organizational team building that may come from company meetings, team lunches, and other gatherings.

## Sprint Demo

At the end of the sprint, everything that was worked on for the current sprint is demonstrated for the team, the product owner, and anybody who's invited to observe. This ritual is called the sprint demo, and it gives all of the engineers the opportunity to demonstrate the stories they've been working on that they consider complete. The sprint demo is the product owner's opportunity to test each story, see if it meets the acceptance criteria, and then either accept or reject it.

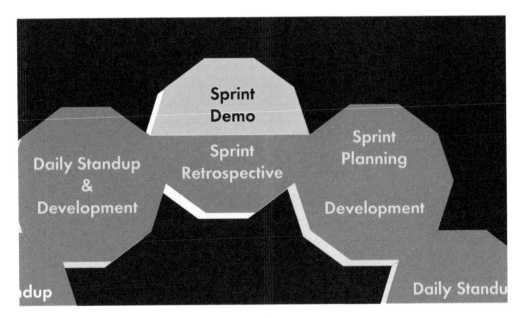

Figure 4.4. Sprint Demo

# Objective

The objective of the sprint demo is to get a clear picture of how much work has been completed during the sprint, and to see what the current state of the product will be after integrating the work that was done during the sprint. Based on the stories that get accepted, the team learns more about how many points they can sustainably accomplish in a single sprint, and this improves their ability to estimate stories and sprint backlogs going forward.

 ### Guests in Sprint Demos

The sprint demo is often a popular ritual for guests, because it's the opportunity for people outside the scrum team to see what the team has been working on, and observe the state of the product in its next iteration based on the latest work produced. But the presence of guests shouldn't be allowed to interfere with the objectives of the ritual, or alter the time box. Guests are observers, not participants. Unless feedback is solicited from guests, they should be asked not to comment on the product or the process.

# Time Box

The time allocated for sprint planning is contingent on the number of stories completed during the sprint, and the level of intricacy associated with the acceptance criteria. Most teams allocate half a day for the sprint demo if they're using a two-week sprint. Once the team has decided how long they want to devote to the demo, the scrum master should be responsible for making sure that everything that needs to happen fits within that time box.

 **Scheduling Demos and Retrospectives Together**

Frequently teams will schedule a sprint retrospective (which we'll be covering shortly) on the same day as a demo. The advantage of scheduling these two rituals on the same day is that the interruption in productivity associated with the rituals is minimized. The disadvantage for the team is that these days produce primarily scrum artifacts, as opposed to tangible product development. That tradeoff needs to be considered, and different teams will have different preferences.

# Preparation

The sprint demo is the opportunity for the team to show off all of the work they've been doing, and demonstrate that all of the stories they've been working on are done and ready to include in the product (assuming they haven't been already). The demo covers all the work back to the beginning of the sprint that has taken a story to the team's definition of done, whether or not that work has been released. Each person who has worked on any stories that are ready to demo needs to be prepared to explain what they did with those stories.

Often the engineers will get together with the product owner before the demo to make sure everybody is aware of what's going to be presented. This can be a useful last step before the demo, because it ensures the stories presented meet all of the acceptance criteria. It also reminds the engineers to make any preparations necessary to allow unreleased stories to be demonstrated.

The scrum master should meet with all engineers who have stories completed, to make sure these stories are prepared for the demo. It's the responsibility of the scrum master to run the ritual, and see to it that everything that needs to be demonstrated can be presented within the time box allocated. The scrum master's agenda for the ritual should include a list of all the stories to be demonstrated, as well as the people responsible for each of the stories.

 **Let the Product Owner Drive the Demo**

While some teams let the engineers demonstrate the stories, a good practice is to have the product owner participate, testing the product live. The engineer who was developing a new feature knows the happy path for the code that will always work. But a product owner will be looking for edge cases, and is aware of the acceptance criteria that are most important. Having the engineer set up the demo, and the product owner present, keeps everybody engaged and ensures that the stories are done to the satisfaction of the product owner.

# Demonstrating a Story

The process of demonstrating each story should be consistent. The scrum master should go through each story on the list, and have the engineers set up the demo for the team. Many teams choose to do this using a projector in a conference room, although it's possible to do this by gathering around a large monitor, or even through remote conferencing services, depending on the nature of the story and the preferences of the team.

At this point in the sprint, the description of the story will be familiar to most of the people in the room, but the product owner should read the story—as well as any major acceptance criteria—to the team while the demo is being set up. That way, everybody will know what to look for, and will be aware of issues that might come up.

Once the story is set up and ready to demo, the state of the product is the main focus of attention. Each story should be a complete slice of functionality added to the product, and the demo should show that slice of functionality in context with the actual product. The demo should walk through each of the acceptance criteria, proving that they have been met.

Sometimes during a demo, it's realized that the acceptance criteria as they were originally written were inadequate, and may not have covered all the cases the product owner needed addressed. If this happens, keep in mind that a demo that meets all of the acceptance criteria—as they were specified in a story that was estimated at the sprint planning—should be considered accepted and done. Any further changes that may be needed are new stories. The product owner in this situation should be prepared to create new stories for a future sprint that relate to the additional acceptance criteria that weren't addressed in the original story.

 **Don't Go Into Detail About Issues Encountered**

While it may be tempting and valuable for the engineers who worked on a story to go into detail about the difficulties or new learnings that came out of developing a particular story, the demo isn't the time for this. If the conversation turns to those topics, the scrum master should encourage people to make a note of these points, and bring them up at the retrospective. Otherwise, the demo can turn into a long dialogue about the details of creating each story, rather than a demonstration of the product with the new stories in place.

# Tallying up the Points

At the end of the demo, a number of stories will have been accepted, and some may have been rejected. The scrum master should add up the number of points completed during the sprint, based solely on the estimated points assigned to stories that were accepted as done. Only stories that were accepted as done, and that were assigned points at the sprint planning, should be included in this total. The total number of points completed in the sprint should be recorded as the team's velocity for that sprint.

Some stories may have been rejected, or may not have been ready to demo despite being included in the sprint backlog. It'll be up to the product owner whether stories that weren't completed will be added to the next sprint, or put on hold pending a possible future sprint. The scrum master needs to keep track of all the stories, both completed and not yet completed, and update their status in any tracking tools that the team may be using.

Often the scrum master will generate a set of reports that are sent out at the end of the sprint demo, updating interested parties about the status of the product. If the team has decided to have both the sprint demo and the sprint retrospective on the same day, the scrum master may want to arrange the schedule so that the necessary data for these reports can be collected between the two rituals, thus making them available for reference.

# Releasing the Stories

Releasing is the process that takes completed features and integrates them into the live product, either so the users can have access to them immediately, or so they can be evaluated for inclusion in a future release. The process may be overseen by release engineers, or integrated at the developer level with a set of fail-safes and rollback procedures.

Web and mobile teams have many options when it comes to releasing. For some teams, releasing a story to the customer as soon as it's completed—sometimes several times in a single day—makes perfect sense. For others, the release process is more complicated, and it makes more sense to group stories from a whole sprint, or even multiple sprints, and do larger unified releases.

**Continuous integration** is an approach that supports releasing stories as they're completed, rather than waiting for the end of the sprint. This usually depends on a robust test suite and an orchestrated set of release scripts. For teams doing continuous integration, the release of the stories into the live product will already have been done as part of completion of the stories themselves, and no further steps will be needed after the demo.

 **Using Continuous Integration**

When a team has chosen to do continuous integration, it's important that the engineers working on a story not abandon that story until it has been released, and demonstrated not to introduce any problems in the live product. While this can result in some downtime for engineers, that time can sometimes be applied to stories related to maintaining and improving the code base.

For teams not doing continuous integration, there will be another task needed to release all the stories from the sprint into production. The tasks associated with the release process are usually considered part of the definition of done for a story, but in this case they may need to be completed after the demo.

Some teams regularly schedule releases at the start of each sprint. Others do releases more frequently, or may release only at certain times of the year, or on a schedule to coordinate with certain events related to the needs of the larger organization or the marketplace. Figuring out how to plan and schedule releases is an opportunity for the team to reflect and iterate on their process, finding the rhythm that works best for them and best meets the objectives of the product owner.

 **Working to a Release Schedule**

Regardless of the actual release schedule, it's important for everyone on the team to understand that what will be released is only what has been completed. Scrum isn't about rushing to finish specific stories in order to meet a predetermined timeline. Scrum is about working at a sustainable pace, learning what the team is capable of, and releasing what has been completed when it's ready.

Any effort to stuff new stories into a particular sprint in order to meet a release schedule should be resisted by the team. If the dates cannot be adjusted, the product owner should be prepared to compromise, deciding what features need to be left out of a scheduled release in order to make time for the team to complete the most critical features.

# Sprint Retrospective

If the daily standup is one of the most iconic rituals of scrum, the sprint retrospective may be the most representative of the agile philosophy. Sprint retrospectives offer the team the opportunity to reflect on what they've been doing at the end of every sprint, and figure out how they want to modify their process going forward.

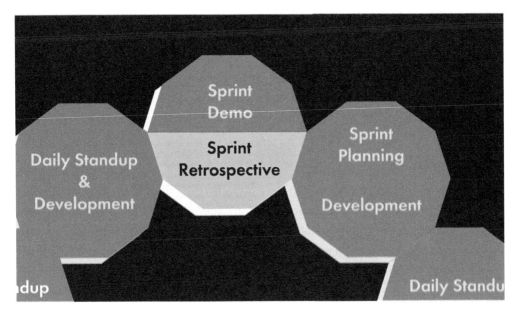

Figure 4.5. Sprint Retrospective

# Objective

A sprint retrospective gathers the team together to consider how the sprint that was just completed went for everybody. During the ritual, everyone in the room will be asked what went well, what didn't go well, and what commitment they're willing to make as a group to improve things in the next sprint. The goal is to come away with a set of modifications to the process that everybody on the team agrees to try for the upcoming sprint.

All the members of the development team, the scrum master, and the product owner are expected to participate in a sprint retrospective. The ritual is led by the scrum master.

 **Guests are Rare at Retrospectives**

Rarely are guests invited to attend the sprint retrospective. This is in order to encourage people to open up about what might have gone wrong during the sprint, and to be candid about how they felt and what issues came up for them. This meeting can be emotional, and the intimacy of a private team environment provides a more supportive context.

# Time Box

Teams may find that the amount of time they spend in the retrospective mirrors the amount of time they might spend in the sprint demo. For a two-week sprint, it's not unusual for the team to devote half a day to the retrospective. When scheduling the retrospective, it's good to err on the side of generosity with the time, to avoid cutting off access to valuable insights from team members.

The amount of time a team dedicates to the sprint retrospective reflects the importance they give to paying attention to their own process, and improving as they go. Some teams may try to limit the amount of time spent in the retrospective. This can come at the expense of communication and improvement. One of the most important aspects of scrum is its emphasis on discussion as a means of enhancing the product development process.

# Preparation

Sprint retrospectives can be highly charged. Everybody involved in the scrum should come to the ritual with some thought in mind about what might have happened during the sprint that they want to comment on. For some people, this can mean creating a long list of issues to raise.

The scrum master should come to the sprint retrospective with an agenda that makes sure both positive and negative feedback is gathered from all participants. It's the responsibility of the scrum master to see to it that everybody has a voice and contributes to the process.

 ## Make Sure the Retrospective Gets Proper Attention

The sprint retrospective is the one ritual that's most frequently shortened, or even abandoned, by scrum teams. That can be a sign that the process in in trouble. Without adequate attention to the retrospective, the team is giving up the opportunity to improve their process. Often the people recommending that this ritual be given less time and attention are the people who are benefiting most from the status quo, at the expense of constant improvement. Making sure this ritual takes place and is given proper attention by everybody on the scrum team is a way of showing care and concern for everybody on the team.

# What Went Well?

The scrum master should ask everybody in the room what they thought went well during the past sprint. This is usually done by going around the room and having everybody report about one or more things they thought went particularly well during the previous sprint. Unless this sprint was a total disaster, most people should be able to come up with something they thought went well[1].

Part of the value of getting people to discuss what went well is to bring people together and give them an opportunity to recognize and appreciate the good work they and their teammates were responsible for.

 **Hold Off on Discussion Until Everyone Has Raised Their Points**

While everybody's participation should be encouraged before the meeting is over, it's not a good idea to allow people to respond, or discuss the points raised, until everyone has had a chance to share their list. The scrum master should provide an opportunity for more open discussion later, but it's most important to give everybody in the team a chance to speak before this deeper discussion starts.

# What Didn't Go Well?

Next the scrum master should go around the room asking people to report what they didn't think went so well during the sprint. This is a more delicate subject, because people may tend to bring up uncomfortable or unpleasant issues.

As before, everyone should be asked to participate. Bringing out honest responses from people about subjects they may feel uncomfortable discussing is part of the skill of a strong scrum master. If somebody really doesn't want to speak, or has something to say that they don't want to bring up in front of the group, they should be encouraged to talk about it independently with the scrum master outside of this ritual.

Saying negative things in front of teammates can feel uncomfortable. Part of the job of the scrum master is to help coach people from sprint to sprint in how to frame

---

[1] One of the reasons this ritual takes as long as it does is because everybody's participation is essential. Nobody should be left out.

their issues so that they can be discussed in a productive way. This ritual isn't about personal attacks, but about finding ways in which the team can work better together.

### Ordering This Ritual

The order of the sections of this ritual—dealing with what went well and what didn't go well—may be reversed according to team preference. Scrum masters may also choose to follow any number of practices to get the team more engaged in this process, including games, note cards, advance submissions, etc. There's a lot of room for creativity in planning this ritual.

## What Should We Do about It?

After everybody has had an opportunity to discuss what they thought went well during the sprint, and what didn't go so well, the floor should be opened for discussion. This is a chance for everybody on the team to say more about the issues they raised, as well as the issues raised by the other teammates, and what they think the team should be doing about them.

For things that went well, the team should try to find ways that the successes can be replicated in future sprints. They might have tried something new this past sprint that turned out to be successful, and that can be integrated into the process going forward.

For things that didn't go so well, the team has the opportunity to discuss what went wrong. Sometimes the issue was that the process was not followed. Other times, the process actually got in the way, and needs to be adjusted. Everybody should be encouraged to give their opinions about changes that might be beneficial.

Eventually, the discussion will circle around to four or five key issues that the team wants to focus on. The scrum master should guide the discussion in such a way that these issues get phrased as revised practices—which the team can then agree to try for the upcoming sprint.

### Only Make Manageable Changes Between Sprints

While there may be many issues discussed, the team should agree on a small and manageable set of changes to make from one sprint to the next. As with user experience testing, the more changes you make between tests, the more difficult it is to isolate which ones were helpful, and which ones caused problems.

By the end of this ritual, the scrum master should present the team with a short and understandable list of changes to the process. Most importantly, the scrum master should poll the entire room, and make sure everybody is in agreement with this set of changes. Then the scrum master should record the team's commitment to the revisions for the upcoming sprint. A team's ability to reflect and improve is as important to its development as the commitment to a sprint backlog is to the product's development.

# Conclusion

In this chapter, we've gone over the four critical rituals for scrum: sprint planning, daily standup, sprint demo, and sprint retrospective. Each of these rituals is repeated once every sprint, except for the standup, which is performed every day.

These rituals take us from feature stories—written by a product owner—through team estimation, commitment to a sprint backlog, working through all of the stories, demonstrating that each story was completed and meets all of its acceptance criteria, to finally reflecting on what worked and what didn't in the completed sprint, so that the team can constantly improve.

Next, we're going to take a look at some of the artifacts of scrum. These tools help a scrum team to understand what they're working on, track their progress, and work together effectively.

# Scrum Artifacts

**Artifacts** are the tools of scrum that allow teams to manage their scrum process. They help team members communicate about the work they're doing, and provide a record of what the team has agreed to do and what they have accomplished. Anyone can point to the artifacts of a scrum team to show people what they're working on, what they've accomplished, and what they expect to be able to achieve.

There are a number of artifacts that help teams prepare and manage as part of the process of working in scrum. Getting familiar with the language of scrum means understanding what each of the artifacts is for, and how it's used. In this chapter, we'll go over a few of the most common scrum artifacts, such as:

- story

- product backlog

- sprint backlog

- scrum board

- definition of "done"

- velocity charts

- burndown chart

- product increment

Different teams have different approaches to how they create and maintain the artifacts they use, but for web and mobile development, some are worth keeping in mind.

# Artifacts Overview

Although formal scrum is agnostic about exactly how the artifacts of the process are used, we'll cover a few ways of building and maintaining artifacts found to be useful for the type of work that web and mobile teams tend to get into.

One of the most basic artifacts of scrum for web and mobile work is the story that describes a feature to be worked on. Stories are developed and managed in backlogs. Separate backlogs are maintained for the product owner to keep track of the overall vision of the product, and for the team to participate in the sprint currently in progress. Both backlogs house descriptions of what needs to happen to take the product forward, but items on the product backlog will not look like stories on the sprint backlog. Scrum teams use a scrum board for tracking the progress of stories through the sprint, and we'll discuss how those work together.

Scum also offers a number of tools for gathering statistics that are useful for tracking the performance of the team, and communicating how product development is going to people both inside and outside the scrum team. Among these, we're going to cover the velocity chart that spans multiple sprints, and the burndown chart that tracks progress within a single sprint.

Other artifacts that a scum team is going to find useful include a definition of done, which is agreed to by the product owner and team under the supervision of the scrum master, as well as the actual product increment, or the current state of the product as it exists at the end of the sprint.

# Stories

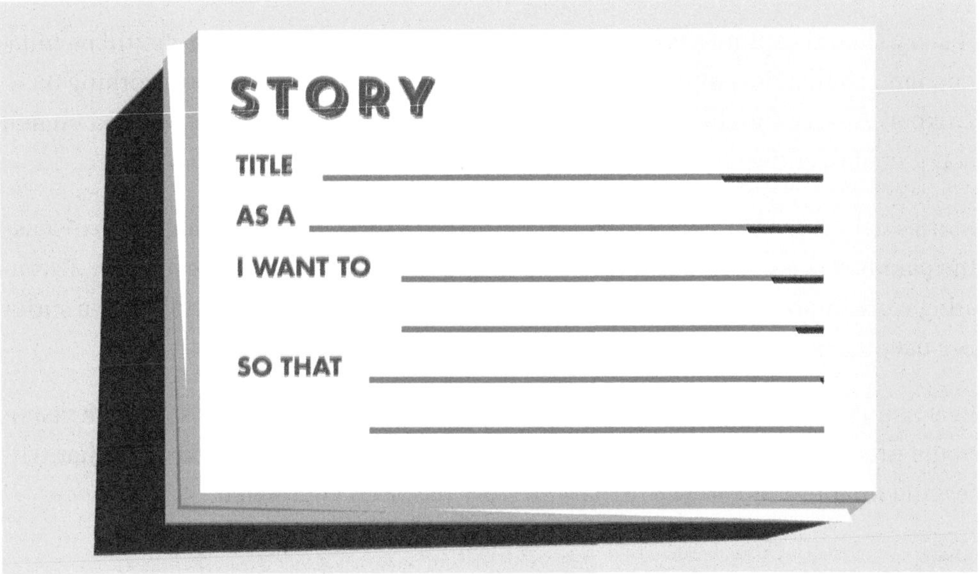

**STORY**

TITLE _____

AS A _____

I WANT TO _____

_____

SO THAT _____

_____

Figure 5.1. Stories

**Stories** are how the product owner communicates to the development team what needs to be developed. Stories are incubated in the product backlog, and then expressed in a standard format so they can be presented to the team as part of the sprint planning meeting to be evaluated, estimated, and then included in a sprint backlog.

## The Origin of Using Stories

The concept of using a story to encapsulate discrete parts of the work comes from Extreme Programming (XP)[1], which is a specialized variation of agile that advocates a number of excellent development practices such as pair programming and writing feature stories. Stories come in very handy when doing web and mobile development with scrum, where the work on a full slice of functionality generally includes many of the same components from the back end to the front end. The team will often see stories that all have the same components, and comparing one story to others the team has worked on before makes new stories easier to break

---

[1] http://www.exremeprogramming.org

down and estimate relatively. For that reason, we're going to consider stories a basic artifact of scrum for the type of work we're talking about.

A story should capture a complete slice of functionality. Each story should be independent, so that developers don't have to complete one story before working on another. A story should be a small slice of functionality that can be worked on and completed over the course of a single sprint.

Stories help capture the essence of a feature, and give the team the ability to discuss the parameters and acceptance criteria in a meaningful and relative manner. Estimating work by sizing feature stories around what the team can accomplish in a sprint is a useful exercise.

Every story should add to the value of the product, and bring it closer to the vision of the product owner. Each story should make it clear how the product owner will test the final product to verify that the story has been completed.

 ## Stories Aren't Technical Specifications

Although new product owners with backgrounds in engineering or product management sometimes feel inclined to work out all the technical issues and propose static solutions with fully fleshed out specifications for every feature, it's important to keep in mind that scrum stories aren't technical specifications. They are opportunities to open a discussion between product owners and engineers about how to implement a feature, and how much effort will be involved. That's one of the reasons stories follow a short and consistent format. It undercuts the temptation to include more detailed specifications.

The responsibility for writing the stories belongs to the product owner. Writing stories that capture the full intention and expectations of the client is a skill that may take time to develop, but it's critical to an effective scrum process. A good scrum master should be able to help coach the product owner in how to write stories that are the right size, express the appropriate acceptance criteria, and open a dialogue rather than close one off.

There's a simple formula that works well for writing stories. People have tried many variations over the years. Through iteration and reflection, different teams may eventually evolve different approaches that work for them, but this is a good place to start:

Name: *brief understandable feature name*

- As a *type of user*

- I want to *behavior*

- so that *justification for the behavior*

Acceptance Criteria:

- Given a *defined state*

- when a *set of conditions or events*

- then a *consistent and testable result*

 **What makes for a good story?**

A good story is short and straightforward. Many scrum teams follow the convention that a story should be able to be written on one side of an index card, three inches by five inches, with the acceptance criteria written on the back of the same card. If it takes more than that much information to write down the story, the specifications may be too detailed, or story may be too complex, and may need to be broken down into multiple stories.

For example, consider a team developing a gallery application. Visitors to the gallery might want to rate the images being displayed, so they can keep track of their favorites. The gallery can function with or without the rating feature, so the work can be isolated as a complete slice of functionality. And according to the engineers, the work involved in adding a rating widget can be completed within a single sprint.

This is how a story might be written so that the team can evaluate it, estimate it, and commit to it in a sprint backlog:

Name: Rating Gallery Images

- As a gallery viewer

- I want to rate the images

- so that I can track and rank the images I've rated

Acceptance Criteria:

▨ Given a logged-in user viewing a gallery

▨ when the user clicks a star in a rating widget for an image

▨ then the value of that star should be recorded as that user's rating for that image

and

▨ Given a logged-in user viewing a gallery

▨ when an image the user has rated is displayed

▨ then the rating widget should reflect the user's previously entered rating

and

▨ Given a logged-in user viewing a gallery

▨ when the "Favorites" switch is toggled on

▨ then only images the user has rated should be shown, in descending order of rating

For a story such as this one, the team may have a standard for how wireframes or designs get attached to stories and communicated. For example, if this is a new widget, the designer may have prepared a mockup and a set of assets that the engineers will need in order to implement the feature. There may also be a style guide or other documentation for the product that needs to be updated with the relevant information.

The story is agnostic about engineering decisions, such as how the API is designed, or what naming conventions are used in the code. While the definition of done for the team may include the need to create documentation about technical aspects such as this, the story that the product owner presents usually doesn't need to have an opinion on these points.

When a story is presented at sprint planning, the engineers should verify that all of the necessary assets and information they'll need have been captured and are available. The actual work to be done in the upcoming sprint is defined by the description on the story card and the dialogue it inspires between the product owner and the team.

# Product Backlog

Figure 5.2. Product Backlog

Stories for the development team emerge from the product owner's **product backlog**. A product backlog keeps track of all the input the product owner has about the direction of the product from the client, along with the research, experience testing, design, and engineering feedback the product owner has gathered.

Unlike stories for the sprint backlog, items for the product backlog don't need to be structured in any particular way. That's because their main purpose is to allow the product owner to keep track of all of the features that are needed. These product backlog items may be quite vague until they crystallize into a clear development story for the sprint backlog. Items in the product backlog should always reflect the product owner's latest thinking about the long-term goals for the product, while the team is working on the specific features for the current increment.

### The Product Backlog is the Responsibility of the Product Owner

While a product owner may choose to share the entire product backlog with the team on a regular basis, the items here are the responsibility of the product owner. It may not be productive to keep reminding the team of items on the product backlog that haven't been touched in a long time, because it will divert attention from the work necessary to complete the current increment.

While many product owners prefer to keep track of items in the product backlog as if they were going to become the final stories, there doesn't have to be a one-to-one correspondence between items in the product backlog and stories that make it into the sprint backlog. Features and requirements that the product owner needs to track may turn into multiple stories, or several items may be combined to create one unified story of the appropriate size and scope for development.

For example, if the customer needs to add a payment system to a site, that may be a single story for the development team, or it may be multiple stories. There may be developer stories around creating the ability to accept payments through a service, and separate stories for accepting credit cards, checks, or even maintaining a token system so that purchases can be made using a virtual currency. It might be possible to develop each one of these independently, and launch the system with just one. Whichever one goes out first may need to carry the weight of implementing some core functionality that all the others will share.

Many product owners find it convenient to track the state of items in the product backlog using a staged process, whereby the item moves from ideation through design through engineering validation, until it's ready to be phrased as a sprint backlog story and added to an upcoming sprint. Product owners should have a clear sense of what it takes to move an item from each of the states to the next, and that should be documented so it'll be consistent for each story.

### Don't Write Stories Until They Are Ready to Be Worked On

It's usually a mistake for a product owner to create development stories for items in the product backlog too long before they're ready to be incorporated into a particular sprint. Items in the product backlog should remain vague enough and flexible enough that they can adapt to changes that emerge out of the iterative agile process of scrum. Product backlog items not worked on for weeks or months can easily become stale, and product owners can easily forget the context they had when writing the story if it isn't worked on soon after it's written. Writing stories in detail too early can often be a waste of the product owner's time, and can lock the team into work that may not be what's currently needed.

# Sprint Backlog

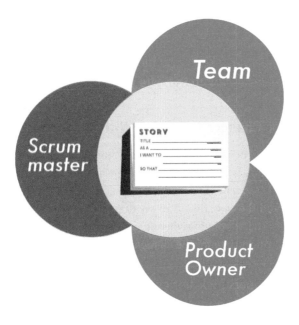

Figure 5.3. Sprint Backlog

The **sprint backlog** is the set of developer stories that the team has committed to working on during the current sprint. A sprint backlog is created as part of the sprint planning ritual, and reflects the shared understanding of the team, the product owner, and the scrum master of what everybody will be working on for the coming sprint.

A sprint backlog consists of a set of feature stories. Each one of these stories emerged from the thinking process that came out of the product backlog, but may not reflect a specific item in the product backlog. The feature stories in the sprint backlog follow the story structure we described earlier.

The size of the sprint backlog for the current sprint is based on the negotiations that happened during sprint planning at the beginning of the sprint. Each story is estimated during the sprint planning, and the backlog as a whole should represent the total number of points that the team believes it can accomplish in the upcoming sprint. Each story has a point value, and that reflects the amount of work the team believes will be necessary to complete that particular story.

The order of the stories in the sprint backlog is established initially at the sprint planning ritual, but it's the prerogative of the product owner to change the order of stories in the sprint backlog at any point during the sprint. The product owner may not add stories to the sprint backlog, or remove stories from the sprint backlog, but may rearrange them as necessary to indicate which stories are most important.

### Making Major Changes to Stories Within a Sprint

If a significant change needs to be made to the stories in the sprint backlog, and that change really can't wait until the end of the sprint, the scrum master should stop the sprint and start a new one, with a new sprint planning ritual. Because of the interruption and the cost, this is a very drastic option. It should only be employed as a last resort, if it's obvious that none of the work being done in the current sprint backlog is appropriate for the changed needs of the product owner.

During the sprint, developers pick stories from the top of the sprint backlog every time that they complete a story and need something new to do. Each engineer should choose the story at the top of the backlog, because that's the one the product owner considers the highest priority in the current sprint. Picking stories that aren't from the top of the backlog will result in work being done out of priority order.

### Working in Priority Order

Because stories are always chosen from the top of the backlog, engineers who have completed their work and are looking for a new story will usually end up taking on stories that aren't in their specialization at some point. This is intentional, as it creates an opportunity for engineers to learn more about the code base, and gain experience outside of their area of expertise.

While it's valuable to have the most skilled talent working on the stories that are most appropriate for their specialties, it's also valuable for a team to share knowledge, so that everyone has a clear sense of what's involved in developing and maintaining the whole product. This helps the team become more versatile, provides learning and growth opportunities, improves everyone's ability to estimate new stories, and prevents mission-critical information from being the exclusive responsibility of one person. Finding the proper balance of efficient development and knowledge sharing is up to each team.

# Scrum Board

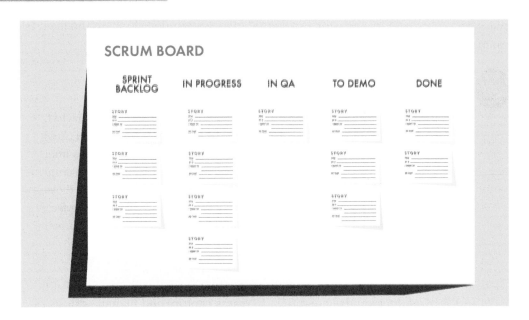

Figure 5.4. Scrum Board

The sprint backlog is often the first column of the scrum board. A **scrum board** tracks the progress of all the stories being worked on in the current sprint until it meets the team's definition of done. Most scrum boards use two or three columns, and move stories from one column to the next to reflect which stories are in the prioritized backlog, which are in progress, which are in QA, and which are ready to be demoed.

Scrum boards provide a focus for the entire team. By looking at the stories on a scrum board during the sprint, anybody on the team should be able to get an immediate snapshot of where the sprint stands, and how the team is progressing toward meeting the goals it set for itself. A good scrum board should be public, so that people outside the team can also take a look and see what's happening, encouraging transparency across the company.

There's wide range of tools available for monitoring the progress of stories through a scrum board. The most basic approach is simply keeping index cards taped to a wall where everybody can see them. For teams that are co-located, this serves a number of useful purposes. Not only does it encourage the use of index cards and handwriting for keeping stories short and succinct, it also creates a natural gathering place for daily standups, as well as a shared visual reminder of where the team is up to.

 **A Physical Scrum Board Carries Risk**

A physical scrum board made of index cards on the wall is subject to abuse, neglect, and possible mischief. People can brush against the board and knock index cards down. Cleaning staff can accidentally rearrange the board. And the changes from one day to the next may be difficult to spot. If you're going to use a physical scrum board, it's a good idea to take photographs of it on a daily basis, and publish those photographs in a place where everybody can access them. This method isn't perfect, but it can provide a recovery system if the board gets disrupted during the normal course of business.

Apart from using a physical board, many companies have developed electronic tools and services that are designed to help teams capture and manage stories as they move from one state to the next. Some of these tools include the ability to track points, generate standard reports, and even set access and privacy levels. There are tools that allow teams to trigger automated build processes in a continuous integration by updating stories. Some tools tie into bug tracking systems commonly used across a wide range of industries, facilitating communication with clients and users. Others tools may simply support the electronic tracking of a story as a card, while allowing everybody to see everything and make any changes.

Among the most popular current online scrum board management tools that allow shared story management and tracking of points, velocity, and various states for each story in progress are:

- Pivotal Tracker[2]

---

[2] https://www.pivotaltracker.com/

- Jira Agile[3]

- Trello[4] (with scrum plugins[5])

Some teams prefer electronic tracking tools so they can be accessed online remotely, or displayed on a large monitor where the team can see it. The field of possible tools is constantly evolving, and any specific recommendations would quickly grow stale as new players enter this fast-moving field. In addition, companies creating these tools have different philosophies about how scrum should work. Those philosophies are reflected in the way the tools are designed.

Changing tools can be a difficult process, and few tools will support direct export in a format that a competing tool can import directly. It's up to each team to decide which tool's philosophy best matches their own approach, and find one they can stick with. A good scrum master should be familiar with the tradeoffs associated with different options.

---

[3] https://www.atlassian.com/software/jira/
[4] http://www.trello.com
[5] http://scrumfortrello.com/

# Definition of Done

Figure 5.5. Definition of Done

We've mentioned the definition of done a few times. The **definition of done** applies to each story in a sprint backlog. Declaring a story to be done is a means of verifying that all of its critical aspects have been completed based on the way each team works.

It's vital for a team to have a shared idea of what done actually means for itself. Teams should create a written definition of done which they maintain as a checklist for every story they work on. This definition should be independent of the documentation for a specific story or project, because the definition of done should apply to the way a team works, independent of what they're working on.

A definition of done is something the team should come up with together. It may be created during the first sprint planning, and iterated on during sprint retrospectives. A team's definition of done may involve radically over time, as the team realizes during retrospectives what aspects of the process may need improvement.

It's not a bad idea to publish the definition of done prominently. This allows people both on the team and outside the team to understand just how much effort is involved in completing any story. This document provides a reference point for questions about whether or not a proposed story is ready to be worked on. If it's impossible for story to meet the definition of done based on the acceptance criteria, having a published definition of done can help the team make that clear.

Usually a definition of done includes a number of familiar expectations. For example, the code should be complete, the build shouldn't fail, the test suite shouldn't be broken, and the product should run as expected. Other points often included in a definition of done include peer reviewing code, writing new unit tests, code commenting, and updating product documentation. Different teams will have different requirements, and the exercise of creating a definition of done is valuable for helping the team realize what's important for every story, not just certain stories.

 **The Definition of Done Must Be Practical**

While it's important for a definition of done to be thorough, it's also important that it's practical. The definition of done must be achievable for every story. There may be practices the team believes should be followed for the sake of the codebase, but which are impractical given the constraints of the marketplace. Usually the engineers will argue for a more thorough scope, while the product owner may argue for a more streamlined approach, depending on the foresight of the product owner and the stability of the market. It's up to each team to make their cases and come up with a definition of done that everybody can agree to before they start working.

# Velocity Chart

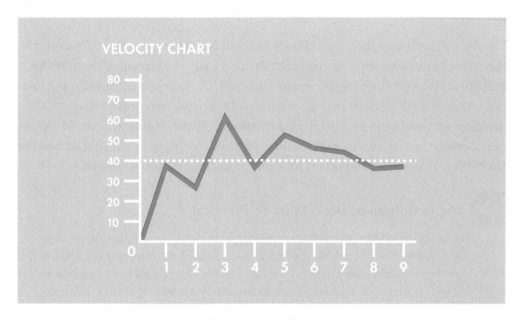

Figure 5.6. Velocity Chart

**Velocity** is how a scrum team measures the amount of work they can complete in a typical sprint. Velocity is measured historically, from one sprint to the next. By tracking the number of story points the team can complete according to their own definition of done, they can build up a reliable and predictable sense of how long it will take them to complete new stories based on their relative point value.

Keeping track of the velocity is the responsibility of the scrum master. At the end of each sprint demo, the scrum master should calculate the number of points that were estimated for the stories that were accepted as done during that sprint. This number should be added as a data point on the velocity chart for that sprint.

Velocity charts tend to start out jumping around from very high numbers to very low numbers, as the team learns how much work they can do in a sprint, and how to estimate stories. The longer a team works together, the better they get at estimating stories consistently relative to each other. That skill leads to a better sense of how many stories, and how many points, the team can accomplish in a single sprint.

Over time, if the composition of the team stays consistent, a velocity chart that started off very erratic will start to find itself averaging toward a consistent value.

Unlike many charts in a business environment, the point of the velocity chart isn't to see a constant increase, but rather to see the values converging around a consistent horizontal line. That line represents the amount of work the team can realistically and sustainably accomplish in a single sprint.

 **Velocity is a Tool for Estimation, not a KPI**

People outside the scrum process may be confused about the nature of the velocity chart. From a management perspective, there may be an impulse to favor an increase in the amount of work a team is doing, and look for velocity to grow over time. But a velocity chart is intended to trend toward a horizontal average. You may hear executives talking about trying to increase the team's velocity, or celebrating a sprint in which the velocity was higher than typical sprints. Get ahead of these conversations by reminding everyone that the point of velocity tracking is to improve the team's ability to estimate how much work they can get done consistently and reliably. A velocity chart that shows a constant increase (or decrease) over time usually reflects a problem in the process.

# Burndown Chart

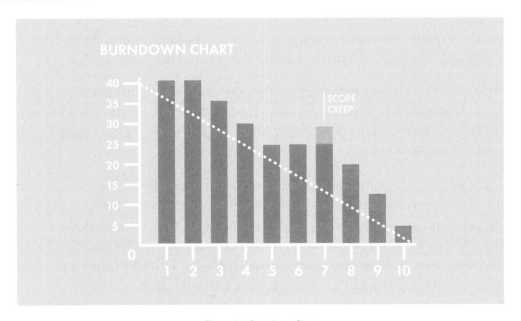

Figure 5.7. Burndown Chart

A **burndown** chart shows the team's progress toward completing all of the points they agreed to complete within a single sprint. This chart starts with the total number of points the team has taken on for the sprint, and tracks on a day-to-day basis how many of those points have been completed and are ready for the sprint demo.

The burndown chart is usually maintained by the scrum master, and may be updated on a daily basis, perhaps after the daily stand up, or on a continuous basis if it's generated automatically by the tools the team is using to maintain the scrum board. The primary audience for a burndown chart is the team itself, although there may be data points on a burndown chart that could be relevant to people outside the scrum team.

A typical burndown chart starts with a straight diagonal line from the top left to the bottom right, showing an "ideal" burndown rate for the sprint. In practice, the point is not to match that ideal, but rather to keep in mind how much of the sprint is left at any point in time, and how much effort the team expects to be able to put toward the development of the product on any particular day of the sprint.

Lines or columns on the burndown chart may be used to represent the number of points of effort actually remaining in the sprint from day-to-day, starting with the number of points the team has committed to at the sprint planning. As work is completed, these columns should become shorter until they reach zero.

Some teams also choose to track the daily work completed, either in story points or in individual tasks toward completing stories. This can be done with a line or stacked columns, tracking these daily metrics against the burndown chart so they can be viewed in context.

There are very few legitimate reasons for a column to be taller on one day than it was on the previous day. If a bug is discovered before the end of the sprint, and a story that was marked as done or ready to demo needs to be worked on again, columns may increase in size from one day to the next. New stories introduced after the sprint has started may also cause one day's column to be higher than the previous day's. A pattern of rising columns on a burndown chart may indicate that the scope of the work is exceeding the originally agreed sprint backlog, which is definitely an anti-pattern in scrum.

**Beware Scope Creep**

The scope of the sprint backlog should be respected by everyone. If new stories are regularly being added to the sprint after the sprint has started, the columns that reflect the amount of work left to be completed in the sprint on any given day may rise above the level of the previous day. This pattern is sometimes represented in a contrasting color, to highlight the fact that the originally agreed to scope may be creeping upward. If this happens frequently, it may reflect problems in the process that are worth addressing in a sprint retrospective.

# Product Increment

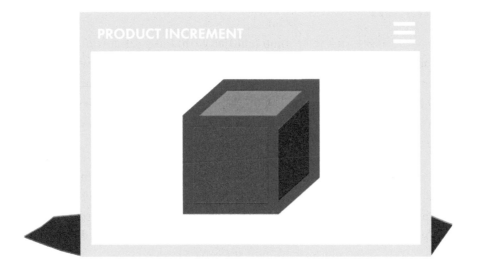

Figure 5.8. Product Increment

The final artifact of scrum is the actual **product increment** as it exists at the end of a sprint, with all of the stories in that sprint which met the definition of done incorporated. At the end of each sprint, the completed features that were worked on should be added to the product for the sprint demo. At that point, the product itself is an artifact of the scrum process.

A goal of the scrum process is to develop features in such a way that the product is in a completed state at the end of every sprint, so it could be released, demonstrated to clients for feedback, or used as a tool for testing. While it's not mandatory for an organization to release the product according to the schedule of scrum, this goal allows the state of the product to be part of the iterative process of development, testing, evaluation, and innovation that scrum encourages.

Ownership of the product increments should belong to the release engineers in most organizations, and should be fully available to the product owner. For web and mobile projects, often the product increment is a live demo branch of the product, maintained in a secure but accessible location.

For teams doing continuous integration, the live site may always reflect the latest work done by the team. In these cases, the public site or app will be the product increment.

## Conclusion

These are a lot of new terms to become familiar with, but getting comfortable with the names and features of the scrum artifacts is a good place to start when learning about scrum. In this chapter, we've gone over stories, product backlogs, sprint backlogs, scrum boards, definitions of done, velocity charts, burndown charts, and product increments. And with that, we've covered the mechanics of scrum for web and mobile development!

Now that we have a handle on the roles, rituals, and artifacts of scrum, it's time for us to take a look at the scrum contract. What is someone agreeing to when they start to work as part of a scrum team? What does it mean to work transparently? How does iterative improvement change the way we approach problem solving? We'll be discussing all these issues and more in the next section.

# 6

## The Scrum Contract

For the first half of this book, we've talked about scrum in the abstract. We discussed what it is, and how it works. We've broken it down into its roles, rituals, and artifacts. But scrum isn't just about the details. Scrum is about the people.

In the next section, we're going to see scrum in action. We're going to take a look at how web and mobile development teams work with the various features of scrum. And we're going to start with the team we've already been introduced to.

## The Beginner's Mind

Starting scrum can feel a little uncertain. There are questions about how it's going to affect the way we work and the way we interact. There are questions about how scrum itself interacts with the hierarchy of the organization. And as we saw in Chapter Two, some people come into scrum with preconceived notions that can limit the potential of scrum.

In later chapters, we're going to do some troubleshooting around problems that can come up for scrum teams. But in this chapter, we're going to discuss what it means to agree to participate actively in the scrum process. Scrum can't work to its full potential without real people participating. Scrum relies on everyone to fulfill the responsibilities of their roles, and scrum makes those roles as lightweight and easy to support as possible.

I like to call this the **scrum contract**. Unlike the artifacts we've discussed before, this isn't a physical contract. It's a mindset that's useful for people to adopt when approaching something like scrum. It doesn't require setting aside healthy skepticism, but it does call for replacing preconceived notions with open-mindedness.

The scrum contract revolves around several key concepts:

- Respecting Roles

- Embracing Transparency

- Maintaining Boundaries

- Iterating Hopefully

- Sharing Definitions

Some of these concepts are familiar to anybody who has ever tried to work effectively on a team. Some of them apply specifically to the way scrum works. All of them rely on a willingness to work together toward a shared goal.

# Respecting Scrum Roles

As we saw in Chapter 3, scrum defines a number of roles for people to take on. These roles serve a purpose in the context of scrum, and everyone needs to understand them regardless of how they relate to a person's position or title in an organization. Scrum isn't about replacing the organizational hierarchy. In fact, scrum tries to be as independent of the organizational hierarchy as possible.

Scrum expects people to be able to distinguish between their job and their role in the scrum process. This doesn't mean that scrum releases you from the obligations of your job. What scrum provides is an alternate view onto the work you're doing. When you assume a role in the scrum project, you're agreeing to participate actively in a shared process to facilitate the work everybody's doing.

Part of assuming a role in the scrum team means being willing to act with your colleagues as an equal around issues that arise during scrum rituals. Anybody participating in scrum should feel free to share their opinions around the project and process, even when those opinions go against the mainstream, or challenge the authority of somebody with a higher position in the organizational hierarchy. When a conflict occurs, it's the responsibility of the scrum master to help mediate and facilitate the conversation.

More fundamentally, participating in scrum assumes a willingness to be part of a team. The roles and rituals of scrum are set up so that everybody has an opportunity, and an obligation, to participate. A member of the team who doesn't share opinions and ideas is letting the rest of the team down. As a member of a scrum team, regardless of your position in the company, your goal is to help support the process for everybody. And because the groups are small and intimate, and the rules of participation are clearly defined, scrum provides a safe space for shy people to experiment with expressing themselves.

Because of the distinction between typical company meetings and scrum rituals, there may be some confusion from time to time about how people are expected to behave. The scrum master should be the ultimate arbiter when questions like this come up. It's up to each team to define for itself what the most useful standards of behavior are, and to enforce them appropriately.

Ultimately it comes down to respect for your colleagues, for the process, and for your place in the process. If you have questions, or you think something isn't working, there's always an opportunity to raise these at the retrospective. Don't miss your chance to participate actively.

# Providing Transparency

For scrum to work effectively, everybody on the team needs to be willing to let other people know what they're working on at all stages of the process. Some call this transparency. It allows everybody to know what everybody else is working on, so that everybody can have a larger sense of the status of the project, and how they can help.

Transparency serves a number of purposes. Part of the value of scrum is that it makes a lot of information about the status of the project visible to anybody in the company, so the people working on the project don't have to be interrupted. By reserving a very short, very clearly defined period of time for the team to update each other on a daily basis, scrum avoids the need for each engineer to face the possibility of interruptions from people who just want to find out what they're working on.

Transparency also allows people outside the engineering team to track the status of issues that may be particularly important to them. Scrum defines sprints in such a way that they cannot be interrupted by new stories, but clients and other people around the organization frequently have changes they want to introduce, and they may see these changes as urgent. The transparency of scrum allows them to see at a glance exactly what the team is working on now, and why those things are prioritized way they are.

The transparency supported by scrum isn't about micromanagement. One of the advantages of scrum is its ability to create as much unmanaged time as possible for the individuals on the team to manage themselves. Nobody knows better than the engineer working on a story what's going to be needed to get that story completed. Scrum provides daily standups as touchpoints for transparency, so that engineers can share valuable insights as they update the team on their status, and then work with minimal interruptions.

Scrum assumes that everybody involved in the process has made the conscious choice to work on a team in the first place. Working together on a team means letting everybody know what you're doing, and being willing to share information and resources. One of the reasons scrum works so well for web and mobile development is that, for the type of work involved in these types of projects, working together toward a shared goal is usually more productive than isolating individuals and trying to coordinate what they produce after the fact.

# Establishing Work Boundaries

Trust is a large component of scrum, and by extension, a large component of working in any type of team environment. We all rely on each other to fulfill our obligations, and support the team process.

But human beings are naturally curious. Any time there's confusion about what other people are working on, there's always a tendency to want to ask questions and explore. Everybody has opinions about what everybody else is doing, and that's the nature of working together on a team. That curiosity is healthy.

However, it's important to remember that people need the space to carry out their work as they see fit. Part of having a role in a group process means allowing other people to have their roles as well. When it comes to scrum for web and mobile development, this means allowing the engineers to work in an uninterrupted way on the stories they have agreed to complete during the sprint. This is part of the self-managing nature of scrum, and it allows for a high degree of individual flexibility, as long as productivity is maintained.

 ## Everyone Needs to Respect the Scrum Roles

This level of respect for the scrum roles needs to extend beyond the limits of the team, or even the engineering organization, in order to provide the needed stability to support an effective scrum process. It's the responsibility of both management and the scrum master to communicate the value of scrum to other people in the company who may have an impact on the expectations applied to the scrum team, including senior management.

On a scrum team, all individuals are expected to fulfill the obligations of their roles, and they rely on each other to do the same in order for the entire process to work. In cases where that process may be breaking down, scrum provides the opportunity for anyone on the team to question how the team is working together at the end of each sprint during the retrospective.

The conversations during a retrospective may sometimes need to dig into the details of individual behavior, which is always a sensitive topic. It's important for the scrum master to allow these conversations to take place when they're relevant to the team as a whole, but to defend individuals from personal attack.

When you work in a team, you can't expect the work you're doing to exist in a vacuum. You need to understand that other people are going to have to touch your work, and that the work they're doing is based on what you do and how you do it. It's a shared context. Sometimes the way you work will have a bearing on the rest of the team, and you need to be willing to allow that to be discussed.

Everybody on the team needs to be able to trust the scrum master to defend their interests. And everybody on the team needs to be able to trust each other to fulfill their obligations. Scrum creates room for that trust to grow, and provides opportunities to demonstrate the value of that trust.

# Honoring Reflective Iteration

One of the most valuable components of scrum is the fact that it adapts constantly as the team, the project, and the context change. No project has a completely predictable trajectory, and this is particularly true of projects in the web and mobile space. So much is changing constantly—not only in the context of the marketplace but also within the teams working on a project—that the ability to adapt quickly is critical.

On a regular basis, scrum takes the time to look at itself and see how well it's performing. Taking advantage of the retrospective, the team has the opportunity to step back from what it's doing and think about how it's doing. Retrospectives not only take the temperature of the team, they provide an opportunity for everybody to share compliments and criticisms about how things have been going, and agree to make adjustments.

Since retrospectives happen every sprint, anything decided at one retrospective is subject to reconsideration at the next retrospective. Any change the team agrees to make in a retrospective should be considered an experiment. You can think of them as tests to be trialed the same way new features on a website or mobile application often are—being evaluated based on real application. It's a mistake for people on the team to think that agreeing to try something at a retrospective means the team has changed its policies permanently.

For example, the team may have noticed that holding daily standups first thing in the morning means that sometimes important people aren't present to share and learn from their colleagues. At the retrospective, somebody may propose moving the time of the standup to immediately before lunch, because everybody is more likely to be present and there's a good chance their flow won't be interrupted at that time. If there's general agreement, the team can agree to try this for a sprint, and then discuss it at the next retrospective to see if the new time actually works for everybody, or if they need to adjust further.

The results of an experiment don't have to be positive in order for it to be successful. That's the nature of the scientific method. If people like a change, they can agree to make it permanent—until somebody brings up a good reason to change it at a later retrospective. If people don't like a change, they have the opportunity to bring that up at the next retrospective, and potentially stop the experiment from going forward.

Reflective iteration allows well-functioning teams to continue functioning and improving, and allows teams with problems to recognize and adjust for those problems. Everything about the process is subject to group agreement. And because there's always another retrospective coming up, there will always be another chance to revisit any decision and shift directions if something's not working.

# Adhering to Shared Definitions

Scrum encourages people to work together rather than alone. In order for that to be productive and not oppressive, people need to agree to shared definitions about the context in which they work. Without a common vocabulary that everybody can agree to, teams would be impossible to manage, and scrum would be of very little use.

Scrum defines a number of new terms for an organization, such as sprint, story, artifact, etc. Part of the value of this is that each organization gets the opportunity to take those new terms and use them in the way that's most effective for them. This doesn't mean breaking from the core standards of scrum, but it does mean coming to a conscious agreement about how each team chooses to operate internally within those definitions.

The vocabulary we're discussing is unique to each team. While shared concepts such as stories, standups, and points may be familiar across all scrum teams, how each team writes a story, how each team manages its stand up, and how each team chooses to assign points are all subjective and constantly evolving properties of that individual team.

For example, one of the things that every team needs to define for itself is the concept of done. One of the artifacts of scrum is a definition of done, in which the team can agree to the standards a story needs to meet in order to move from development to acceptance. Unless everybody has a clear understanding of what it takes for a story to be done, there may be disagreement about how to work on a story, and what needs to happen at each stage of the process.

Scrum doesn't attempt to define done for the team, but scrum expects the team to create and share their own definition of done that everybody can agree to. Scrum provides loose guidelines, and allows a great deal of flexibility for the team to define their own standards, so they can discover their own path to sustainable productivity.

# Summary

Working on a scrum team requires willingness. Everybody needs to be willing to take on the roles required of them to keep the team productive, to be transparent about the work they're doing, to respect the boundaries that define everybody's roles, to work together to iterate and improve the process regularly, and to agree to share definitions for how everybody will work together.

With these concepts in mind, in the next chapter we're going to take a look at a particular team working on a particular project. It's the same team we met before, from the WithKittens.com site, but now they're starting to work as part of a scrum team. We're going to show how new stories for that site develop from ideas in the product backlog, and how the team goes about evaluating those stories to see if they make sense, and how much effort they'll take.

Chapter **7**

# The Lifecycle of a Story

We've gone through scrum in detail, talking about the roles, rituals and artifacts necessary to keep a scrum team running smoothly. We've discussed the attitudes of the team members, and the concerns people have when coming into scrum. Now it's time to start looking at the actual scrum process.

To do that, let's start at the very beginning. In this chapter, we're going to meet a product owner, and learn how the idea for a change in an existing web and mobile product can go from general thoughts, to specific user expectations, to stories ready for the team to work on.

We've already started talking with the folks on the WithKittens team, and we're going to keep working with them. We'll discuss what the product looks like to start with, and what changes the product owner decides to introduce. Then we'll see those changes crystallize into full stack slices of functionality for the team to estimate and deliver.

As we go through this process, keep in mind that this team's approach to implementing the details of scrum may be different from your team's approach. For example, each team has its own relative scale of points, and has to adhere to its own definition of done. The important things to keep an eye on are the fundamentals that we've discussed in the previous chapters.

 **Why isn't scrum standardized for every team?**

You may be asking why scrum isn't simply standardized for every team. One of the advantages of scrum is that each team starts with a shared set of general concepts, and then iterates toward the process that works best for them. That usually results in a fairly consistent definition of done, but it varies depending on the development and deployment context for each team. For example, points are completely relative to the tasks the team actually tackles, so they can vary wildly from team to team.

# What's WithKittens?

The WithKittens team consists of six engineers, one product owner, and one scrum master. They've been working together for about three years, with a little turnover, and have produced both a website and a mobile application designed to add pictures of kittens to any image uploaded by their clients.

Most of the users of the service stay in a free tier forever, merely adding kittens to their own social media images and sharing them, which promotes WithKittens thanks to embedded text that overlays the generated images. But this is also a critical service for some customers, who pay handsomely for the privilege of knowing only the very best kittens will be added to their images consistently and reliably, with a great deal more control over the quality and content than free users get. Making these paying clients happy, and making sure their service is rock solid, is what keeps the lights on and supports users on the free tier.

The team's expertise includes image processing specialists, back-end data processing and API management engineers, front-end engineers for both web and mobile interfaces, as well as billing and security experts. The product owner has a background in product management for both desktop and web applications, as well as a few years of experience in front-end engineering. The scrum master has worked in both product and project management.

In addition to the core team, there's a dedicated designer on the Design team who works with the product owner on the service, as well as a pair of QA engineers who report to a different manager, and a small team of DevOps engineers who keep the site running and also handle IT issues.

A lot of what the team does might be familiar to any web or mobile development company, such as user management, security, and billing. The unique facets of the service include details such as figuring out the ideal positioning of kittens in pictures, as well as the best ways to optimize images for proper delivery.

# Why Just Kittens?

The founder and CEO of the company has a long history of working with cat rescue societies. The idea for the service began as something to support one local nonprofit organization, and grew quickly as other nonprofits—and eventually users—decided they also wanted to be able to add kittens to their pictures.

Most of the paying customers for the service are high-end social media users, as well as people who want more control over the way their kittens are presented in their pictures. But there's also a growing business clientele, including companies in marketing and promotion who use the WithKittens service to add appeal to their materials.

Because of the popularity of kittens in general on the internet, the company's focus on kitten-only content has never been a serious issue before, although it's been the subject of some discussions. Until now, any questions about plans to expand beyond kittens have always been brushed off with vague references to to the company's historical focus on cat rescue, and the importance of kittens to their ever-growing user base.

## Client Desires

The one place in the company where the push to expand beyond kittens has been strongest is from the sales department. Some members of the sales team have felt that their ability to grow the market has been hindered by the fact that they can't target companies looking for puppy-related content.

Recently, the head of sales sat down with one of the company's largest clients, a multinational marketing conglomerate, and learned that they were planning to switch contracts to a competitor of WithKittens over this question. The following excerpt from an internal sales memo highlights the issue:

> We've been supporting [redacted] for more than a year, and haven't had any complaints about the service. They currently account for over seven percent of our revenue. But they keep asking us why they can't add puppies to their images. Puppies are just as cute and just as common on the Internet as kittens, and they want to be able to appeal to a broader audience. We're running out of excuses. Our competition supports adding baby animals of all types, even though we know they can't match us for quality and control. But that won't matter if we can't be more flexible. If we can't satisfy [redacted]'s needs, we're definitely going to lose them.

This memo catches the attention of the company founder, who reluctantly calls in the product owner for a meeting. Among the issues they discuss are the value of adapting to changing market expectations, and the appropriateness of adding a service that conflicts with the historical intent of the company—not to mention the company name.

Together they decide they need to do some work on puppy-friendly features—if just to figure out what it might take to support puppies in addition to kittens, given their current infrastructure. Among the critical issues they feel it's important to keep in mind are the overhead of maintaining an entirely independent service, versus the cost of developing and supporting an integrated service.

Because of the urgency of the sales memo, they decide this is a high enough priority that it has to bump their critical seasonal push to integrate the new Persian and Angora kitten promotion for the holidays, which the team is scheduled to work on next. The product owner goes back to the head of product with the details of that discussion, and receives approval to make that change to the prioritization.

## Product Backlog

With a fresh mandate, the product owner goes back to the product backlog, where all future ideas for the service are tracked. It's almost painful to push some of the other high-priority ideas down on the list, but it's clear this is going to have to be done first.

After a day or two of research on competing services, the product owner pulls together the details of the idea. Most of the other services put the animal choice late in the process for customers, almost as an afterthought. Following that approach, if they are going to offer customers the choice of puppies as well, instead of just kittens, that will require a major adjustment to the core product, as well as a new interface element.

There are only one or two other services that focus exclusively on one type of baby animal. For the most part, they are small and haven't gained the market traction that WithKittens has managed to achieve. But despite the potential for fragmenting the market, there is an advantage to being able to stay focused on kittens on their core service. It also avoids the confusion of adding puppies on a service called WithKittens.

Ultimately, the product owner decides the best approach will be to ask the team to clone some sections of the WithKittens service, and create a minimal parallel WithPuppies service. They have already purchased the domain WithPuppies.com in anticipation of this possibility, and the designers have been playing with ideas around this concept casually.

Before moving forward with that decision, the product owner calls one of the senior engineers in for a chat, and confirms that this would be the more technically straightforward approach. The sooner they can get a service into the market that they can test, the sooner they'll know whether or not it makes sense.

## Formulating a Feature

After sketching out a few ideas, the product owner decides the best way to do this quickly and efficiently will be to create a scaled down version of the product exclusively for web users. The company can use its deployment testing system to limit the audience to a small percentage of visitors.

These visitors will be presented with a link that offers to show them puppies instead of kittens as soon as they log in. If they click that link, they'll be taken out of the WithKittens.com domain and put into the with WithPuppies.com domain. There, the experience of the site will be the same, except kittens will be replaced with puppies.

Since this isn't what most customers came to the company for, it will have to be very easy for a visitor to switch back to kittens. It would also be great if they could include a way to gather feedback from visitors.

## Lining up Design Resources

The product owner checks the queue of projects the Design team is working on. Design is set up under a kanban process, so it will be possible to slot in the new design story to start immediately after the designer finishes whatever is currently being worked on.

After sitting down with the designer and discussing some of the visual and user experience issues implied by converting the site from kittens to puppies, the product owner creates stories for design around changing image elements and kitten-specific cues in the content creation path of the application. There will need to be some copy changes as well, and for the sake of this test, the product owner will write those.

The designer agrees that there won't be much need to change the overall user interface. There is already a feedback gathering tool that they can skin for this purpose, as well as an alert banner format that can be used as a trigger for visitors who want to convert back to kittens from puppies. Other than that, it will just be a matter of populating a database with appropriate puppy images, and adding subcategories to the existing menus.

The designer confirms that it shouldn't be necessary for all the design elements to be completed before the engineering work starts, because the specifications for the image content and the text changes should be driven by the standards already in place for the site. As long as the changes stay within the parameters that already exist, this work can probably be completed within a single sprint from a design perspective.

# Writing Stories

With the go-ahead from initial consultations with Design and Engineering in place, the product owner sits down to write feature stories around the idea of creating a parallel WithPuppies site. The team is used to working in two-week sprints, and the objective is to see if it will be possible to define the scope of this story narrowly enough that it will fit within a single two-week sprint.

# A Full Slice of Functionality

There are a few ways to break this feature apart, but the product owner doesn't want to get into the weeds of trying to do the work the engineers are better at. The goal is to stand back and view this as a feature from the user's perspective. How would a user who wants puppies instead of kittens take advantage of this feature?

The best way to describe what will be needed—in terms of stories the team has worked on before—is by creating additional pages in the content creation flow. These pages will be skinned versions of existing pages, with different options presented. They will use the existing alert and feedback features, and will only be triggered for a percentage of visitors.

Thinking this through, the product owner can anticipate some of the questions the engineering team will be likely to ask when presented with this story. The acceptance criteria for the story will need to be specific about what percentage of visitors will be tracked to this new experience, and also provide information about the availability of design and copy changes.

# Story Format

The product owner writes up the following story to present to the team, describing the new puppy feature:

- As a logged-in user who has been selected for the puppy beta

- I want to be able to opt-in to view puppy-specific options during the content creation process

- so that I can have the benefit of including puppies in my content

Some of the main acceptance criteria for the story go like this:

- Given a logged in user who is randomly (five percent) or explicitly assigned to the puppy beta

- when that user is viewing the content creation pages

- that user should be shown an alert banner offering to include that user in the puppy beta and

- Given a logged-in user who has opted in to the puppy option

- when that user views the content creation pages

- that user should see puppies instead of kittens in all of the options, and a customized feedback form, and an alert banner with an opt-out link

and

- Given a logged-in user who has not opted in to the puppy option

- when that user views the content creation pages

- that user should see the standard kitten site with no indication of puppies or a puppy beta

# Presenting and Estimation

The team has been working with scrum for several sprints, and is just done with sprint ten. At the end of that sprint's demo, there are several stories that have been completed. The shared electronic scrum board the team relies on to keep track of their progress looks something like this:

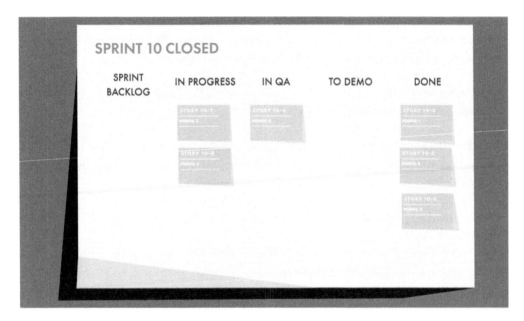

Figure 7.1. Sprint 10 Closed

There are two stories still in progress, and one that has been completed but not yet approved by QA before the demo. All the other stories from that sprint have been accepted at the demo, and are now done. The team has completed eleven points during sprint 10.

In preparation for the planning meeting to kick off the next sprint, the product owner works out the copy changes that will be needed for the puppy story, and creates a document in a shared repository where the design assets will also live.

After explaining the background of the new story to the team at the sprint planning ritual, the product owner reads the full story out to everybody, and asks for feedback.

One of the first questions from the engineers is why the puppies can't be integrated into the existing site, instead of being separated out. Another engineer answers before the product owner has a chance, pointing out that integrating a different type of animal would make managing the data much more complicated.

"But won't the customers be confused when they come to a kitten site and get taken to a page without any kittens?" the first engineer asks.

"It'll be just as confusing if they get offered kittens and puppies on a site that's clearly just about kittens," the second engineer replies. "Besides, the whole navigation is built around kittens, including the URL scheme and the API."

"Yeah, what about the URLs?" the first engineer asks the product owner. "Everything about our site says it's about kittens."

"We'll have to handle that with messaging," the product owner says. "This is a limited test, and people who opt in will have to do so intentionally, understanding that this is a beta."

"Are all those edge cases handled in the copy?" the first engineer asks.

"Yes, I have messaging written for all of those conditions, and I plan to make myself very available to the team in case things come up while working, so we can address them without interrupting progress."

At that point, the scrum master asks, "OK, does everybody know enough about the story that they feel comfortable estimating it?"

There is a moment or two of silence as the engineers look around at each other, and then the first engineer who had spoken before says, "I think we need a little more clarity on the scope of this."

## Defining Scope

"So how is this going to affect the experience of the rest of the site?" the first engineer asks. "I see that the user who's chosen to see puppies will only see puppies on this particular page, but what about on the rest of the site?"

"The scope of the changes will be limited to the pages being changed," the product owner explains. "That means the test users might experience a visual disconnect when they leave these pages and navigate to other parts of the site, such as the billing and confirmation pages. After all, we've got a lot of kittens and kitten-related themes running through all the pages. But it's out of scope to make broader changes to the entire site just for this test."

"Is there something else we can do?" another engineer asks. "We have the alert only on these pages. Can we have them on the rest of the site as well?"

"I'm worried about making changes that will affect people not involved in the test," the product owner says. "I don't want to make this any bigger than it has to be, and I certainly don't want to put the stability of the site as a whole in danger."

"I don't think it would be that hard," the engineer goes on. "We already have the ability to turn on an alert that can be shown on every page of the site. Remember, we did that during the last holiday promotion."

"Can we make sure this will be limited to the people who opted in?" the product owner asks.

"Sure, that won't be a problem," the engineer replies. "In fact, we could even make it so that the people who are selected for the test could opt in later, if we wanted to."

"I don't think that would be necessary," the product owner says. "Let's try to do this as simply as we possibly can."

In the end, the product owner decides that it's sufficient if visitors who have opted in to the puppies retain the alert about the puppy beta at the top of the page as long as they are in puppy mode. It will be there to remind them that they have selected puppies instead of kittens, despite the strongly kitten-oriented messaging on the rest of the site. That change is added to the acceptance criteria, which now include a line looking like this:

- Given a logged-in user who has opted in to the puppy beta

- when that user visits any other page on the site

- the alert banner at the top of the page should be present, reminding them that they're in puppy mode, and allowing them to opt out

At this point, another engineer points out that visitors who have selected puppies, and created content using puppies, could lose what they have created if they opt out elsewhere on the site.

"It depends on how we implement it," another engineer says. "But it'll be awkward to keep the custom elements available for people who have opted out of puppy mode."

"What do folks think would be easiest?" the product owner asks. "Should we try to retain mixed content, or should we force people to delete custom content if they disable puppy mode?"

After a little bit of discussion, the team decides that the best solution to this will be for the opt out link on the alert to take people to a page warning them that any puppy-related content they have created in that mode will be lost when they opt out. This will be an inconvenient but appropriate action for that page during the beta, regardless of whether they've arrived there from the content creation section, or from elsewhere on the site.

To handle this, the product owner changes the acceptance criteria around the opt out link:

- Given a logged-in user has opted in to puppies

- when that user clicks the opt-out link

- that user should be taken to a confirmation page warning that they'll lose any puppy-related content if they opted out

"Does that look good to everybody?" the product owner asks.

There are nods of agreement from all around the table. One or two of the engineers say "Yeah."

"Great!" the scrum master says. "Let's vote."

# Debating Effort

The team has chosen to use a modified Fibonacci scale to estimate points. That means relative estimated points for a single story can be one, two, three, five, eight, thirteen, or twenty. Everybody on the team has a deck of cards with those numbers on it, and when the scrum master calls for a vote, each of the engineers shuffles through and picks the card that represents the amount of effort they think this task will take.

"We've got five thirteens and one twenty," the scrum master reports. Historically, this team assigns twenty points to stories that they don't believe can be completed within a single sprint. Even thirteen-point stories are questionable. "Do you want to tell us why you think this would be a twenty?"

"It seems to me like there's a lot of unknowns," the engineer who voted twenty says. "This is the first time we've tried to do something like this, and I know our database is pretty tightly integrated with the whole kitten concept."

"Yeah, you've got a point," one of the other engineers says. "We've been talking about re-factoring out the kitten terminology for a long time, and it's never been a high enough priority for us to get to it."

"Do we really need to do that in order to make this happen?" the product owner asks.

"The code is going to look really ugly unless we do," the first engineer replies.

"I get that," the product owner says. "Is it bad enough that we can't do it just for a test?"

"It's just frustrating that we don't get a chance to re-factor these things when stories like this come up," the first engineer says. "We've been talking about this technical debt for months, and we all know it has to be addressed at some point."

"I hear you," the product owner says. "I do understand we need to make some time to clean things up. I'll support making that the next highest priority in the next sprint after we get this completed. Can the team write up a chore for that, so we can keep track of it and not keep pushing it down to the bottom of the pile?"

"This story would be a lot easier if we did that refactor first," the engineer says, grimly.

"I understand that," the product owner says, "but we don't have that luxury right now. If we can get this prioritized, maybe the issues that come up as we work through this story will help define how the refactoring needs to go. Is that a possibility?"

The engineer shrugs. "We'll see."

"OK," the scrum master says, "can we agree to move forward with this story as a test—if we get the assurance that the re-factor will be the next top priority after that?"

"I can agree to that, I guess," the product owner says.

The engineer nods, and the scrum master goes on, "So does this still feel like a thirteen to everybody, given what we just talked about?"

"I don't think the code'll be bad enough for a twenty," another engineer says. "We can stick it in a separate branch, and use explicit naming conventions. As long as it's tagged properly, it'll be easy to back out."

"Then I guess I can go with thirteen," the first engineer says.

"Great," the scrum master says. "Then this is a thirteen, and we still need somebody to take responsibility for writing up the re-factoring chore."

"I've got it," the first engineer says, still frowning at the product owner, who nods in agreement. "And I'll be sure to bring it up at the retrospective, to make sure we commit to it like we agreed."

## Agreeing to a Sprint Backlog

The product owner doesn't have any new stories to introduce other than the one about the puppies. That makes establishing a prioritized sprint backlog much easier. Using the team's numbering convention, that story is labeled **11-1**.

There are a couple of stories that haven't been completed in the previous sprint, and one that's still in QA. The product owner decides it's more practical to let the engineers working on those stories to finish them instead of pulling them off and making them work on the new story first.

The sprint backlog includes all the points for the stories that weren't completed the previous sprint, along with the new thirteen-point story. The total goal of 24 points is a little high, given the team's previous velocity average of 18. But in this case that total includes several points from stories already partially completed, so the team agrees that it is feasible.

The engineer who argued that the puppy story should be estimated at 20 points plans to set aside time to write up a chore for the refactoring that's needed, so it can be introduced as soon as possible.

Once the sprint backlog is complete, the scrum master makes sure that everybody in the team agrees to it, and that the product owner will be satisfied with the product increment represented by those stories. Then, with everybody in agreement, the scrum master launches the sprint.

Here's what the sprint backlog looks like at the start of sprint eleven:

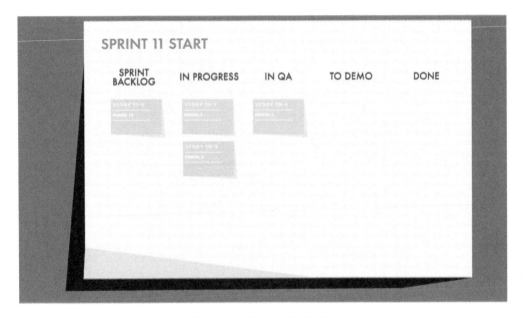

Figure 7.2. Sprint 11 Initial Backlog

# Summary

So not everything has gone perfectly smoothly, but when in life does everything go perfectly smoothly? On real web and mobile development teams there are often long-overdue refactorings that need to be considered, personality differences, conflicts of interest, and genuine disagreements over the details of what needs to be done next.

Scrum isn't going to make these things go away, but it provides processes for working through them in a professional and productive manner, and for discussing them openly so that the process can be improved every sprint.

In this chapter, we've seen a new requirement show up on the product owner's desk, pushing existing plans for future development down, and forcing a discussion about technical debt in the codebase. But the team has been able to evaluate the story, estimate it, and commit to it based on the modified acceptance criteria.

In the next chapter, we'll see the team work through the sprint and tackle the new puppy story. We'll find out whether they can actually complete it within a single sprint.

# Chapter 8

# Working Through Scrum

In the last chapter, we were introduced to the product owner's world, and taken through the process of developing and creating a story for the team. We saw how requirements were gathered, how the product backlog was built up, and how the expectations of internal and external clients, along with other interested parties, translated into clearly defined scrum stories for the team.

Then we went through the process of seeing how stories are introduced to the team, and how the team estimated them. We watched as the team negotiated with the product owner to make sure that what they were going to work on made sense, and was capable of being finished within a sprint.

Now it's time to follow that story through a sprint. In this chapter, we're going to see how the team divides up a large story like the one we've been discussing into smaller tasks, and distributes these out so they can all be worked on and completed. We're going to see how all aspects of the story get addressed until they meet the definition of done.

Finally, we're going to see the team go through the demo process with the product owner, and with any luck, maybe the story will be accepted at the end of the sprint.

Either way, there's certainly going to be a lot to discuss at the retrospective. Let's find out what happens.

# Working Through a Story

By the time the planning meeting has ended, the team has committed to a new sprint backlog. As you may recall, the scrum board currently looks like this:

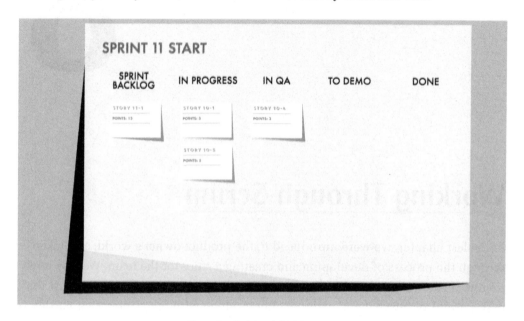

Figure 8.1. Sprint 11 Initial Backlog

The new story for creating a test version of the site to support puppies, labeled 11-1, is high on the priority list, but it's a little lower than some stories that are still in progress from the previous sprint, but haven't been accepted yet. That's a compromise the product owner is moving to make so that the team won't lose momentum on stories that are almost completed.

## Taking Ownership

The next morning, the team has the first standup of the new sprint. As usual, the team goes around the circle, with each engineer reporting on what they've done since the last standup, what they're planning to do until the next standup, and whether they have any blockers. The first three engineers still have cleanup work to do from stories they've failed to finish in the previous sprint, and they have no blockers. But the fourth engineer, the most junior on the team, doesn't have any work left to do, and is available to take on a new story.

"Looks like I get to take the big one," the junior engineer says nervously. There's some humorous cheering from the rest of the team.

"OK, we're putting your name on it," the scrum master says.

"I guess I'll start tasking it out," the junior engineer says, "but I'm gonna need some help. Does somebody want to pair with me?"

"Sure, we can work together," the next engineer says.

"Great," the scrum master says. "So you two are a team, and you're working on this story. Got any blockers yet?"

"Just the usual sense of intimidation," the junior engineer says. "But I guess we've got this."

## Defining Tasks

The first thing to do when taking on a big story is task it out. This means defining the individual subtasks that can be worked on in parallel, so that the story doesn't get trapped in one person's head. Some teams prefer to split stories into tasks during the planning meeting, but this team has decided that the person who takes ownership of the story will also be responsible for breaking out the tasks.

Depending on the preferences of the team, tasks can be written just like stories, or they can be written as technical specifications more appropriate for sharing ideas among engineers. Tasks can also be entered into a number of scrum board tracking systems, so they can be tracked and assigned to different people as they go through development, review, and QA.

The pair of engineers responsible for the puppy story works through the sub elements that will be necessary to make the story a reality. It takes several hours, and they have to call in the product owner a couple of times to clarify points. By the time they're done, they've broken out more than six tasks, each of which will need to be done before the story can go to QA for final testing.

Together, they write up the descriptions of the tasks and add them to the electronic scrum board the team shares. Another advantage of having the tasks available on the board is that team members who aren't directly responsible for the whole story can still take responsibility for a task, so the work can get done more efficiently. This also had the advantage of spreading the knowledge about how the story is implemented around the team.

When they are done adding the new tasks to the scrum board, it looks something like this:

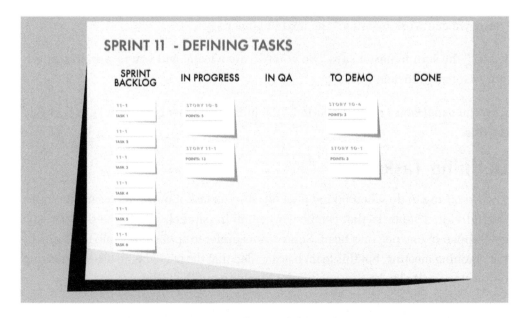

Figure 8.2. Sprint 11 With Tasks

The engineer who's taken ownership of the story makes a point of alerting QA about the state of the tasks. After talking with QA, they discuss the testing plan, and decide on some standards for how the tests should be evaluated to match the acceptance criteria of the original story. In this case, it is agreed that QA will be involved in testing the pieces of the story while all of the components are being completed. Getting QA involved ahead of time gives them a chance to start writing the tests early.

# Tracking Progress

Once all the tasks have been defined, the initial pair determines the priority order of the tasks, and decides which task they think needs to be done first in order to support the development of the rest of the tasks. Between them, they feel that they have the skills necessary for the first task, so they assign themselves to that task, and set to work developing the necessary code without calling in additional help.

At this point, they move the first task for the puppy story to the in progress column:

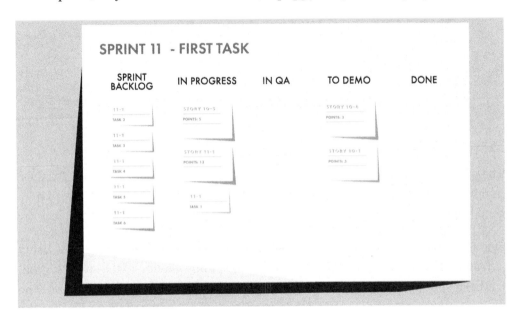

Figure 8.3. Sprint 11 First Task

A little later, one of the other engineers on the team completes a story, goes over it with QA to make sure it's complete, and is then free to start working on new stories. The engineer checks the board, and sees that several of the new tasks from this high-priority story have not yet been started. After checking in with the first pair to make sure there won't be any overlap between the tasks, the engineer takes ownership of the next highest priority task in the top story, updates the scrum board, and gets to work.

Once the second task is in progress, the scrum board looks something like this:

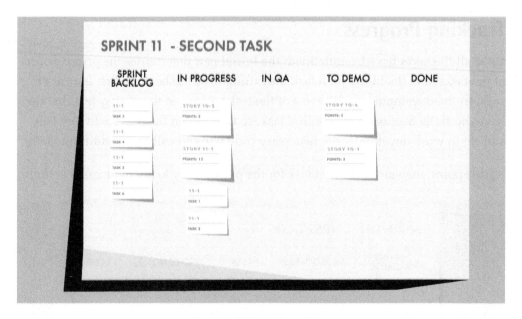

Figure 8.4. Sprint 11 Second Task

The product owner is following up as well, doing some work on the copy for the puppy story, and checking in with Design on the status of the assets. Now it's a good time to check the scrum board to see what's going on.

One story that was in progress and not yet completed in the last print is now listed as ready to demo. The new story for creating the puppy version of the site is started, has been split out into six tasks, and two of those tasks are already in progress. The product owner makes a mental note to check up on the status of the tasks after the standup tomorrow.

Before the end of the day, the scrum master checks on the status of the stories on the board. The new tasks have been added, and the format is clean, which means the team working on the puppy story has followed existing conventions correctly. There doesn't seem to be any need to interrupt the engineers who are working on their stories.

## The First Standup

The next day at the daily standup, the QA engineer responsible for the puppy site story attends, and makes note of the status of all of the tasks. The product owner attends as well.

**Attendance of QA in Standups**

Some teams consider QA as core team members, but for the WithKittens team QA is not required to participate actively in all team activities. It's entirely up to the people not directly on the team whether or not they will attend a standup. WithKittens QA attends standups only when alerted that new tasks or stories might be discussed. The product owner likes to be at all the standups when possible. Of course, neither QA nor the product owner speaks until after all the engineers on the team have reported on their status. Even then, the scrum master limits them to statements of relevance to the whole team.

The first to report is the junior engineer responsible for the puppy story, who explains how they have broken the story into tasks, and how they have begun working on the first task.

"We'd appreciate any feedback on the task breakdown," the junior engineer says. "I think we addressed all of the acceptance criteria, but the more eyes we have on this the better I'll feel."

"So you'll be working on this task for the rest of the day?" the scrum master asks.

"Yeah, I think we will."

"Any blockers?" the scrum master asks.

"I don't think so," the junior engineer replies.

"No, I don't think we have any blockers," the other engineer on the story agrees. "We should be working on this at least until tomorrow."

"Great," the scrum master says, making a note to follow up on the request for feedback, and then continues around the circle until everybody has reported. Then the team is dismissed, and the engineers go back to their various projects.

After the standup, the product owner checks in with the scrum master and the people working on the tasks for the puppy story, and lets them know that the design work has been started, and the copy updates they discussed at the planning meeting are in the repository. None of the tasks that require design assets have been started yet. Based on the updates from the standup, they probably won't be started until the designer has everything ready.

# The Second Standup

On the second day of the sprint, the product owner and the QA engineer both attend standup again. All the engineers are present, and nobody has any blockers for the stories they're working on. As the scrum master is just about to dismiss the team, one of the engineers speaks up.

"I have a quick question about how this puppy story is going to work with the help pages on the site," the engineer says. "I was thinking about it last night, and it's going to be confusing for people in the beta if there's nothing on the help pages that explains what the beta is, and how to get back to the regular site."

"That's a good point," the product owner says. "Do you think that's something we can handle with the plans for the custom header?"

"I'm not sure," the engineer says. "The header's currently not structured to show up differently on help pages."

"Is that something you think would be easy to add?" the product owner asks.

"I wouldn't count on it," another engineer says. "The way the site is structured, the help pages are served separately from the rest of the content."

"That's right," the first engineer says. "It's going to be a tricky one."

"Do we need the whole team here for this," the scrum master asks, interrupting the conversation, "or can we take this offline?"

"I don't know," the product owner says.

"Yeah, we can take this offline," the first engineer replies.

"OK, great," the scrum master says. "In that case, the standup is over."

As the rest of the team steps back to their desks to continue working on their projects, the scrum master comes over to the product owner and the two engineers, who are talking about the help pages.

"Should the three of us discuss this now, or do we want to follow up on this later?" the scrum master asks.

"I think I see what the problem is," the product owner says. "I can write up a story that addresses the way I think it should work."

"Are we going to add that as a new story?" the scrum master asks.

"It feels like scope creep to me," the first engineer says.

"No, I think it's covered by the acceptance criteria for the original story," the product owner says. "These are pages on the site, and they need to be handled just like any other pages on the site."

"Let's check the acceptance criteria and make sure," the scrum master says.

Together, the four of them go over to a computer, pull up the scrum board, and take a look at the acceptance criteria for the story as the team has estimated it. In fact, the acceptance criteria do say that the changes in the header to support beta users of the puppy site need to accommodate all of the pages on the site, without distinguishing the help pages.

"Well, that's going to be a tricky one," the first engineer says.

"Do we need any further details about how it should be implemented once we have the updated text from the product owner?" the scrum master asks. "Or can one of you take on writing up the specifications and adding this task to the board?"

"I can do it," the first engineer says, a little glumly. "But it sure feels as if this might add more effort to the story than we expected."

"Yeah," the second engineer agrees. "I don't think we estimated this one with enough points."

"Well, we can't change the point estimate now," the scrum master says. "Just another data point. We'll have to do what we can."

"Does that mean you don't think you're going to be able to get this story done by the end of the sprint?" the product owner asks.

"We'll have to see," the first engineer replies.

The four of them stare at the story's acceptance criteria for a moment. Then the scrum master asks, "OK, are we all good? Don't forget to tell the story owner about the task you're adding."

They all nod and return to their jobs. After a few hours, the new task is added to the scrum board by the engineer who accepted that responsibility, and the board looks like this:

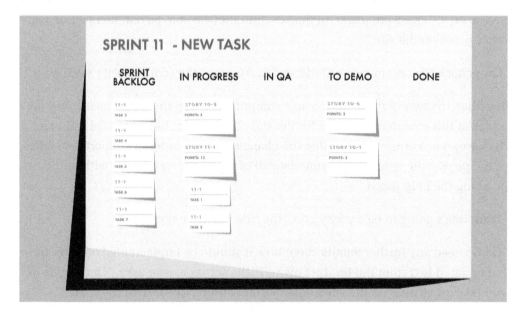

Figure 8.5. Sprint 11 New Task

# The Rest of the Sprint

By the end of the sprint, most of the team has swarmed onto the puppy story, but not much else has gotten done. Design has finished the flow for the front-end user experience and the image assets, and works with the engineers to make sure they're integrated appropriately.

While the team is working on the code, QA is developing the tests necessary to validate it. QA also meets with the product owner a couple of times to clarify acceptance criteria. Eventually, each of the tasks moves across the board from *In Progress* to *To Demo*.

**Using a Third Engineer for Code Review**

> Since many of the tasks in this story are worked on by pairs, a third engineer has
> to be involved in doing the code review. Not every team requires code done by
> pairs to be reviewed by a third engineer, but this team has included that as part
> of their definition of done.

Despite the need to support the help pages, the team manages to finish and review
all of the code to their satisfaction. Because of the unusual naming conventions
they need to adopt in order to distinguish this code from the rest of the site, there
is some confusion during code reviews. That slows down development a bit, but
not enough to prevent the junior engineer who took ownership of the story from
handing it off to QA for a final check before the end of the sprint.

The definition of done for this team includes both code review and QA, as well as
client acceptance. Because QA has been integrated with the team from the start,
they've been building the test suite throughout the sprint based on the acceptance
criteria.

Most of the tasks for the story have produced reviewed code that can be unit tested
independently as they're completed. Now it's a simple matter to run the integration
tests and verify that the features work as expected from start to finish. If the story
is accepted and pushed to production, these tests will be added to the universal
suite for the site.

# Demonstrating the Story

A day before the demo, as part of the preparation, the product owner sits down with
the junior engineer who owns the puppy story. They have already walked through
the various components a number of times during the sprint, but the product owner
wants to be sure all of the acceptance criteria can be demonstrated.

"Will we have this staged properly on production-ready servers in time for the
demo?" the product owner asks.

"Pretty much," the engineer replies. "That's the server QA has been testing on. It
should be fine for the demo."

"Do I need to know anything special," the product owner says, "or can I just go to the same server we're using right now?"

"We shouldn't need to set up anything custom," the engineer replies. "I think you've been through the components a few times already. Once it's deployed, you should be able to join the beta, test the features, and then exit the beta successfully."

"Can I go through the whole thing right now?" the product owner asks.

"Not yet," the engineer replies, "but QA has passed on everything, so we just need to go through deployment before tomorrow. It should be ready in time for the demo."

"Great, I'm looking forward to seeing it," the product owner says.

## Checking Acceptance Criteria

At the demo, everyone is in attendance, including the QA engineer and the designer who has worked on the puppy story. There's a lot of curiosity about how this is going to turn out. The scrum board shows all the stories that have been in progress for the sprint are ready to demo:

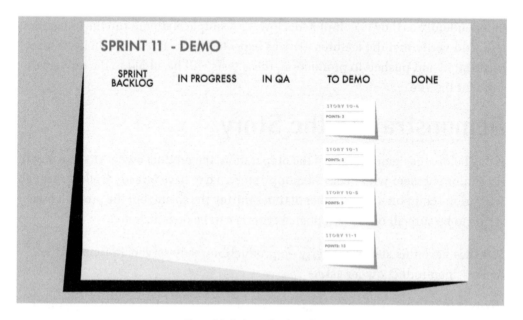

Figure 8.6. Sprint 11 Ready to Demo

### What happened to the tasks?

All of the tasks that have been broken out for the puppy story are no longer relevant, and so have been hidden from view on the scrum board for the demo. Once a story has been completed, it isn't relevant to the product owner what it took to get it done, only whether the entire story meets all the acceptance criteria. For the sake of the team, the individually defined tasks are still stored for later referenced if needed.

The first thing the product owner does is verify that the stories carried over from the previous sprint are now completed. After walking through those, and verifying that all of the acceptance criteria have been met, it's time to demonstrate the big story that has taken most of the time during the sprint.

"So, how do I get into the beta?" the product owner asks.

"You should have a sample invitation email with a link to join the beta," the junior engineer responsible for the story replies. "Check your inbox, and click the link to get started."

The product owner checks the email, and confirms that it matches the text that was provided. It looks very basic, but it does meet the acceptance criteria. The designer starts making notes.

Clicking the link in the email brings up a custom login page with the invitation message, which also meets the acceptance criteria. After clicking the accept button, the product owner logs in, and starts navigating around the puppy-friendly version of the site.

The top of the page shows the alert header, just as it was defined in the acceptance criteria for the story. "So far it looks pretty good," the product owner says.

"We had to take some liberties with the formatting in the header to accommodate the help integration," one of the engineers points out. "I don't think the solution is ideal, but it does get the job done."

"Yeah, let's check that out now," the product owner says. A few clicks, and the screen changes to show the help pages on the site. The header expands on these pages, revealing additional help topics for the beta that aren't covered in the standard help screens.

"That seemed to be the best way to get the information you needed up on the screen where people might expect to find it," the engineer says. "If we had had time to do the full refactor, we could have integrated it directly into the help topics, but there just wasn't time to do it with the code the way it was."

"That doesn't look great, but I see where you're coming from," the product owner says.

"I think we can come up with some more elegant ways to do that," the designer says from the back of the room. "I can work on some sketches."

"That would be good," the product owner says. "I really don't want to send it out looking like this."

"But it does meet the acceptance criteria, right?" the scrum master confirms.

"Yeah," the product owner agrees. "So if we do want to do updates for the visual design, that'll be a new story for the next sprint, right?"

"That's what it sounds like," the scrum master says.

After reviewing the rest of the features, and going through all of the acceptance criteria, the product owner identifies a number of areas where there's room for improvement. The team has made some expedient choices on visual layout in order to get all of the functionality in place.

Not all of the interface options were specified in the design comps, and some features were outside the scope of the existing style guide. The designer now takes notes, and confirms with the product owner that they'll go over these issues after the demo to discuss what needs to be worked on next.

But despite some visual lack of refinement, all of the boxes have been checked. For the sake of the scrum process, the team can consider the story completed, even if it isn't yet ready for production release. So the scrum master updates the story on the scrum board and sets the status to done. This updates the point count, adding all the points for the story to the total for that sprint.

By the end of sprint eleven, the team has completed all 24 points in the sprint backlog, and the scrum board looks like this:

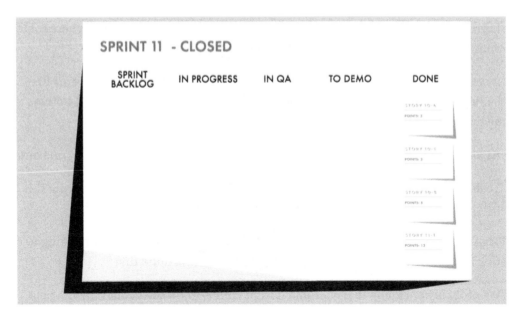

Figure 8.7. Sprint 11 Closed

# Sprint Retrospective

After the demo is completed and the sprint is closed, the team sits down with the scrum master to go through the sprint retrospective. The point is to get people talking about what they think went well during the last sprint, what they could have done better, and what changes they think they should make to the process going forward.

"One thing I think went really well was having the opportunity to follow that big story from start to finish," the junior engineer who took responsibility for the puppy story says. "It gave me a great chance to see how our architecture works from top to bottom."

"You did a really good job on it," the engineer who had paired on that story says. "I learned some things about our own architecture that I didn't know, too. There's some really messy stuff in there."

"Yeah," another engineer says, "that's one of the things I think didn't go so well. I really think we should have had the chance to do the refactoring before trying to build this all out."

"I agree," the second engineer says. "But now at least we have a sense of where some of the mess is, so we know what to focus on first."

"It would have been easier if I had just been able to dive in and fix that stuff first," the third engineer says. "I already knew where most of it was, and it still bothers me that we did it backwards."

"At least now you're not the only one who knows," the second engineer points out.

"Yeah, but it sounds as if we're not going to get a chance to do the refactoring this sprint, either," the third engineer says, sounding grim.

"That's how it sounded to me too," a fourth engineer chimes in. "They're going to stick in the stories to get the design changes for the beta done first."

"We probably are going to have some design stories to fix the visuals for the beta," the scrum master says. "But the product owner did agree to give us time for the re-factor as a top priority if we finished the story, and we did. I'll follow up on that before the planning meeting to make sure."

"Well one thing," the third engineer says, "is that I want to go through those new designs with a fine-toothed comb and make sure they're really final before we estim-ate them."

"Should we make that another goal for the next sprint?" the scrum master asks.

The engineers around the room nod. At the end of the retrospective, they came up with a short list of improvements they wanted to make to their process, as well as a couple of tasks for the scrum master to follow up on with the product owner.

The two points everybody can agree on are that working across the entire stack has been frustrating but also useful for exposing issues in the code that need to be fixed, and that the priority for the next sprint should be getting those issues addressed. One way or another, it's going to be an interesting planning meeting going into the next sprint.

## Summary

One of the things we've learned about scrum is that it can't give you the team that you might wish to have, but it can help you optimize the resources that you have available, and support them in working together effectively. In this chapter, we've gone through how a team with some challenges approached a new story that stretched their resources.

- We saw how the team organized the work, and broke a big story out into engineering tasks so that it could be developed in parallel.

- We watched the team encounter issues with the acceptance criteria, and get feedback from the product owner about how to address them during the sprint.

- We saw the compromises that came up during the demo, and how they led to revised expectations for the upcoming sprint.

- And then we listened to the team go through their concerns at the retrospective, discussing what went well, what could have gone better, and what they hope to see in the next sprint.

Implicit in all of this is the philosophy of collaborative transparency and self-management behind scrum. In the next chapter, we're going to discuss how to make scrum work for your team. We'll talk about how to introduce the concept of scrum to an organization, what resources are needed to support scrum, and also how to address some of the anti-patterns that can show up when learning to apply scrum.

Chapter

# 9

# Making Scrum Work for Your Web or Mobile Team

For most of this book, we've been talking about the practicalities of scrum. Although the core definition of scrum is very versatile—supporting a wide range of applications—we've gone into a fairly opinionated and detailed explanation of the mechanics of scrum as it can be applied in web and mobile teams. (Many of these principles and practices, however, apply just as well to other kinds of development work.)

Now that we have some shared vocabulary and concepts, in this chapter we're going to discuss how to get a team started with scrum. We'll go into more detail about the arguments for scrum when doing web and mobile development. We'll discuss what scrum is best for, how it compares to the alternatives, and provide answers to some of the questions that come up when making the case for scrum and applying it in a company.

# Taking Steps Toward Scrum

We've learned some things about scrum, and how scrum can help your web and mobile development project. The next question is how to take your team from zero to scrum. That's going to be different for every team, and you'll need to evaluate your own situation to determine just how ready the organization is to adopt an agile approach.

## Buy-in

If your organization is currently following something like a waterfall process, the people at every stage in the cycle may be comfortable with the roles they have, and won't be anxious to try something new. You may need to show them just how much more effective and productive the organization could be with a scrum-based process.

Executives may be concerned they'll have less control over a team that self-organizes, and that they'll have less input into a process that generates its own ideas. Point out to them that an agile process gives them the opportunity to shift and adjust priorities every sprint, adapting to the marketplace more effectively, while providing valuable feedback that they can use to help guide their decision-making process.

Engineering managers may be confused about what their role is in a team that manages itself, but that concern grows out of a semantic misconception about the concept of a team being self-managing. Managers are still essential to help the team allocate resources, resolve personal issues, and identify and retain talent. Managers also bring their own background and knowledge to the whole development process. Engineering managers are free to dedicate a portion of their time to hands-on work as one of the engineers on a team, but their main responsibility is securing the team's place in the organization, making sure they have the tools and resources they need, and defending them from distractions so they can continue with their scrum process.

Designers may wonder how they're going to fit into a scrum process, when their work doesn't necessarily follow the same cycle as the rest of the team. Show them that scrum provides designers with increased opportunities to have more impact before decisions get made, because designers can be involved in every stage of the development, and participate from the planning stages all the way through release.

Engineers may be concerned about the change in their roles, especially if they've gotten used to doing one thing very well. Agile puts a greater responsibility on each engineer to play a broader role on the team, but it also opens up new opportunities for learning and growth. The stability provided to engineers by commitment to a sprint, and the confidence that the requirements they've agreed to won't change until the sprint is over, may be strong selling points in an organization where interruption and chaos have been a problem.

Adopting agile isn't a one-way conversation. The champions of scrum should listen, and learn from the concerns of the people who are going to be asked to change their approach during this process. For everybody, it's useful to remember that scrum is always an experiment that's just going to last for the length of the next sprint, with the opportunity at that point to revisit and change anything that doesn't seem to be working. Sometimes the experimental nature of scrum is one of the most compelling arguments for giving it a try.

## Training

Although scrum isn't that complicated, and can be described pretty thoroughly in a book, it's invaluable to have the team trained by someone from outside the organization who understands agile.

An objective, third-party trainer can step into an organization and see problems in a way that a person inside the organization may not be able to. A good trainer will also be able to coach people through some of the more subtle or complex aspects of the process, making sure they have a full understanding not only of what they're doing, but why they're doing it.

Scrum training can take one or two days for the entire team, and may be best done off-site, in a neutral place where people won't be distracted by the day-to-day work currently going on. Don't try to shortchange your organization by giving them less training than they need. It's too easy to start applying the labels of scrum to a process that's anything but agile.

 **Do Not Use Scrum as Simply a New Way to Describe Existing Processes**

It's a mistake to think of scrum as a new way of talking about an existing process. Scrum isn't just a set of fancy vocabulary words. There are teams that start using scrum tools without proper training, and end up following the same broken process that hasn't worked for them in the past, while applying labels such as "sprint" or "story," or having hour-long daily "standup" meetings. Don't let your team be one of these.

Getting everybody's active and focused participation is important for the scrum training to take root. Anybody who isn't properly trained may not understand how scrum is supposed to be applied, and that can lead to frustration and confusion that's easily avoided with a little preparation.

The list of people to invite to the training should include some representatives of senior management, as well as all the people in the organization who are going to be participating in the rituals on a daily basis. You don't have to get everybody in the company trained, but anybody whose role involves direct interaction with the scrum team is a likely candidate.

## Staffing

It may not be necessary to hire anybody new in order to implement scrum in your organization. Most of the roles in an agile team can be filled by people who already exist in the organizational hierarchy.

A product manager may be a likely candidate for the product owner role on a scrum team. Engineers—whether junior, senior, or management—should all be considered equal on the development team for the sake of scrum, despite the differences in their ranks in the organization. Often QA engineers are also included in scrum, which provides a number of benefits in terms of redundancy, cross-training, and organizational reach.

Project managers may be the best people already working in the organization to step into the role of scrum master, with some training about the differences between the skill set involved in managing projects versus running scrum. In a pinch, any member of the development team can be trained to act as scrum master. However, a good scrum master may be the best new hire to make when implementing scrum.

Somebody who understands how scrum works, and is familiar with the issues that can arise, can smooth out the rough edges more easily than a person just getting up to speed with the process. It's less important for a scrum master to be familiar with the type of work you're doing than it is to have someone good at coaching people through the scrum process.

# Tracking Effectiveness

Scrum is all about establishing a sustainable process that adds real value, and reviewing that process on a regular basis in order to make sure it's producing the desired results. So why not use agile techniques to make sure scrum is working for your company?

One of the most useful techniques when implementing scrum in a new organization is to establish a baseline of productivity before scrum, and use that to measure the effectiveness of scrum. Where you establish that baseline, and how you measure it, are very subjective. Each organization has its own standards and productivity indicators.

For example, a web development team may judge itself based on the number of comparable features it's able to add to a website. A mobile development agency may track how quickly they're able to get from concept to implementation with a typical client. The ability to fix or address bugs may also be relevant. Ask around, and find out how the company currently judges its own performance. (You may be surprised at how little formal attention is paid to the matter.)

Before implementing scrum, pull together a representative sample of data about the performance of the organization without scrum. That way, you'll have a comparison point to use when evaluating how effective scrum is, and reporting on it to interested parties. Keep updating the data as the team applies scrum and develops its agile abilities.

If you don't see improvements, you can use the scrum process to raise the issue during a retrospective, and figure out what's working, what isn't, and how you can improve.

# Troubleshooting

It would be lovely if everything just worked as you expect it to perfectly, from the beginning to the end every single time. That doesn't happen in the real world. One of the advantages of scrum is that it doesn't pretend that things are always going to be perfect. Scrum has built-in checks and balances to make sure the team is always responding appropriately to changing conditions, and reinforcing scrum techniques to make sure they support their goals.

Scrum breakdowns tend to follow familiar patterns across organizations. Let's take a look at a few of the aspects of scrum we've discussed, to see where issues are likely to crop up, and how to address them.

## Undefined Time Boxes

When a team is starting out using scrum, they may not understand how much time to allocate for their rituals. Defining a time box in which the ritual must be completed helps focus everybody's attention, and shows respect for the team's time. There's a temptation for new teams unsure about how much time to allocate to leave the time box undefined for the various aspects of the ritual.

It's especially important when teams are starting out to define time boxes explicitly for every aspect of a ritual. Sometimes these time boxes may just be guesses, and the team will need to learn by iterating from sprint to sprint just how much time they need. It's better to propose a wildly incorrect time box and try to enforce it than it is to leave the time box loose. The exercise of proposing and enforcing time boxes demonstrates respect for the team's time, and respect for the process.

There are some experts who advocate reducing the length of time boxes to the minimum length possible when teams start exceeding their time boxes consistently, and then working closely with the team to help them get through all the stages of each ritual within the very limited time that's been allocated. This helps establish the importance of defining and respecting the time box for each aspect of the ritual. And if the team mentions at the retrospective that the time box was too short, it can be extended by consensus for the next sprint.

## Optimizing for Sprints

There comes a point at the end of many planning rituals when the team is agreeing to a backlog for the sprint. At this stage, the product owner should already have organized into priority order the stories that have been estimated, and considered what would make a sensible increment for the product at the end of the sprint.

As estimated stories get moved into the sprint backlog, the team discusses how much work they believe they can get done that sprint. Often, the last story added to a sprint backlog will not be large enough to bring the team up to their projected velocity based on their historical performance. At that point, the team may try to negotiate with the product owner about the order of the remaining stories, in order to get a story with the optimum number of points added to the sprint backlog so their commitment exactly matches their expected velocity.

This unwise exercise is optimizing for the sprint, and it demonstrates a basic misunderstanding of the point of scrum. The prioritization of the stories, and the purpose of working on them in order, is about adding value to the product, not pushing forward an agenda around optimizing the scrum process. When it comes down to it, the work is more important, not the number of points completed in a sprint.

It's better to leave that sprint backlog a little short, and agree with the team that they may start work on the next highest priority story once all the stories they committed to in this sprint are done. After the commitment for the sprint backlog is completed, it's perfectly fine for the team to start working on a story of any size that has the next highest priority, even if they don't expect to complete it within the same sprint. Ultimately, the team's point velocity is estimated across multiple sprints, and it will all average out.

## Long, Lazy Standups

The purpose of the daily standup is to capture the heartbeat of the team, for the sake of the team. These rituals are kept short in order to respect everybody's time. One of the first mistakes teams tend to make is to treat the daily standup as if it were a team meeting. This could be played out in many ways, including having the team sit for the daily standup, planning announcements at the beginning of standup, and not limiting cross-talk during standup.

Everybody is expected to stand during the ritual, so that nobody feels inclined to let the ritual exceed its time box. No devices or other distraction should be in anybody's hands, and nobody should be working on their laptop or talking about anything other than the story currently being discussed.

It's a slippery slope if you start allowing people outside of your team to include announcements at the beginning or the end of standup. Announcements tend to encourage more discussion, and that can quickly lead to standups that last longer than 15 minutes.

There should only be one person speaking at a time during the standup, and that person should be the engineer discussing what was done since the previous standup, what will be done by the next standup, and whether there are any blockers. Issues will come up that need further discussion, but that discussion needs to be taken off-line for follow-up after the standup is completed. Everyone on the team should feel empowered to support the scrum master in cutting off other conversations and keeping the standup focused.

# Work Interruptions

One of the premises of scrum is that the engineers will have the opportunity to plan ahead for the duration of the sprint, without worrying that their work is going to be interrupted by distractions and side projects. The team commits to a sprint backlog, and it's up to everybody to defend the integrity of that backlog and not allow additional work creep in.

The reality—particularly for web and mobile development teams—is that things come up. Servers go down. Features break. Time-critical announcements happen. Users get confused by new features and they need to be adjusted. Urgent issues need to be addressed that were not anticipated when the sprint began.

In traditional scrum, any change to the stories committed to in the sprint backlog demands that the team stop the sprint, go through a new planning ritual, and establish a new sprint backlog. This is considered a draconian measure, and has been put in place to discourage anybody from violating the integrity of the sprint.

Web and mobile development teams need to incorporate a certain degree of flexibility into their process, due to the dynamic nature of their work. It would be very impractical if the team had to start a new sprint every time a broken form needed to be fixed, or a press release needed to be edited. But there's a balance that must be maintained. It would be just as inefficient if part of the team had to drop everything and start working on a new, urgent feature every time an executive or a client got a brilliant idea for a new feature.

It's the nature of web and mobile work that the team needs to be flexible enough to deal with emergencies, but they also need to be strict about what constitutes an emergency. This is something the scrum master, the product owner and the team should define explicitly as part of the team's scrum contract.

Any new work pulled into a sprint should be expected to reduce the team's velocity. That additional work should not be estimated, since it was not part of the team's sprint backlog commitment. If the team starts allowing new stories to creep into a sprint on a regular basis, that will pull them away from their backlog commitment, and will be reflected in their velocity.

Making time to address urgent issues is essential, with the understanding that urgency is a concept everyone on the team needs to agree on. If the integrity of the sprint seems to be broken too regularly or too casually, it's something the team should definitely be discussing during the retrospectives.

## Loose Demos

Every team needs to come up with a clear definition of done. Part of that definition should always include meeting all of the story's acceptance criteria as it was written. This gets tested during the demo. It's important to be consistent about the way stories are accepted at demos, and not to allow the standards to get too flexible.

One common issue that comes up is teams that allow stories to be accepted when the acceptance criteria are not fully met. Sometimes, stories are accepted into a sprint, but the work on them lingers into the beginning of the next sprint, because they were "almost done." This confuses the end of one sprint and the beginning of the next, making it more difficult to say clearly what was done in one sprint, what needs to be done in the next one, and what the team's real velocity is.

It's also vital that teams come to demos prepared to demonstrate all the work they did in the sprint. Frequently, teams find themselves sitting around waiting while the developer finishes deploying code, or adjusting the staging environment for the demonstration. While it's reasonable to expect that there are sometimes emergencies that get in the way, it's the responsibility of the developer who worked on the story to make sure it's ready to demo, and that the product owner knows how to walk through the demonstration.

Some teams take a very strict approach to this, not accepting any story that isn't an exact fulfillment of all of the acceptance criteria and ready to demonstrate at the start of the demo. While that may seem harsh, the important thing to remember is that getting things into the sprint is not as important as getting the work done.

Teams can be as severe or as lax as they like around their demo acceptance criteria, as long as they're consistent. There's nothing wrong with erring on the side of being severe, and making sure that what was done in the sprint was completed within the sprint. The critical issue is to make sure everybody agrees to the process and understands the importance of following it.

# Problem Solving During Retrospectives

Without retrospectives, scrum doesn't have the opportunity to learn from its mistakes, or benefit from its excesses. Retrospectives also serve a strong team-building function, in that they allow the team members a chance to share what's on their mind with their colleagues. While the most common problem teams have with retrospectives is not holding them at all, next on the list would be trying to resolve the problems that come up during a retrospective at the ritual itself.

Retrospectives are an opportunity for everybody on the team to bring up anything they think went well or didn't go well during the previous print, and to discuss how to address the issues going forward. This touches on potentially sensitive topics, and can bring a lot of emotions to the surface. For people who feel they may be on the negative side of a discussion, there's a strong impulse to try to resolve the problem then and there.

There are several reasons why a retrospective is not the best occasion for resolving issues that come up:

- Some issues may involve too many of the people in the room, and may require more consideration before everyone can agree to a solution.

- Not everybody is going to feel comfortable talking openly at the retrospective about some issues that may be sensitive, and that might be better addressed in smaller meetings.

- It's also easy for people who have louder voices or stronger opinions to take over large group discussions, negating opinions that might be easier to recognize in a less open form.

- In addition, trying to solve a problem that doesn't affect everybody in the group is a waste of some people's time.

It's up to the scrum master to remind everybody that the retrospective is not an occasion for solving problems, but rather for recognizing that they exist, and for then committing to solve them during the upcoming sprint.

It's reasonable to allow the conversation around a problem to go on for a little while, so that people have the opportunity to fully understand all sides of an issue, and commit to finding a reasonable resolution during the sprint. But if that discussion gets too deep into the details of how to solve the problem, it may be time to cut the discussions short out of respect for everybody's time.

## Summary

In this chapter, we've gone over some of the steps that a company may want to take as it starts to implement scrum.

We talked about getting buy-in across the organization, both from within engineering and outside. We discussed how to get the team trained, and what a trainer should be expected to do for the team. We talked about the staffing issues, and how the people who already work in the organization can adapt to take on the roles of financial process. And we talked about the importance of tracking and measuring the effectiveness of scrum. We also dug into some of the problems that can come up as a team gets used to scrum, and how to work around them.

In the next chapter, we'll get back in touch with the people we met in Chapter 2, now that they've been working for a while in a scrum environment, and find out how well their concerns have been addressed, and how they're adapting to the scrum process.

Chapter **10**

# Adapting to Scrum

We've talked about the systems that make scrum work. We've discussed the approach that scrum takes to product development, and some of the rituals and artifacts that help the people taking on the roles of scrum to get their work done efficiently and effectively in a sustainable manner.

But ultimately, *scum is about people.* If the people on your team aren't feeling inspired and motivated by their work, scrum can't step in and change that. What scrum can do is help people who are good at their jobs work together in a more efficient and effective way, while constantly improving.

Way back in Chapter 2, we were introduced to everybody on the team, and we got a chance to discuss some of their concerns about scrum. So let's take a look now and see if they've learned enough to help them address those concerns.

# A Senior Engineer

## Initial Concerns

I came into scrum worried about buzzword management. I've seen too many companies where they threw around words like agile without really understanding what they meant. Some people treat agile as an excuse to have more meetings. Maybe meetings make them more comfortable. That doesn't work for somebody like me, because I have responsibilities that can take hours or even days of uninterrupted time to get right. I didn't want managers hovering over me, pulling me into lots of meetings, and shifting my focus, getting me distracted from the thinking that's involved in doing my work.

## What I've Learned

The ideas of scrum are good. The important thing is to carry through on them. The time we spend now in meetings that don't have to do with agile has been greatly reduced, and that's a big relief. When somebody needs to talk with me, I can point to exactly what I'm working on, and explain if I'm too busy and why. And if somebody suddenly comes up with a change they think is urgent, I have a whole team around me willing to stand up for the sanctity of the sprint, so we don't have to adjust what we're working on while addressing this new issue.

At the same time, it's easy for people to see who's working on what, so all the questions don't end up coming to me. Now there are more people on the team getting experience with the parts of the code that I used to be responsible for 100%. That frees me up to do some of the long-term thinking, and apply my knowledge to reviewing the work of other people who are still learning some of the lessons I've had to learn over the years.

## What Still Frustrates Me

It can be hard to plan and architect a project when you're not sure what direction it's going to take next. For example, there are aspects of mobile development that require longer time frames than a single sprint. Sometimes we have to develop in layers, always thinking about what could be considered a complete slice of functionality every sprint.

Technically, it can be a challenge creating an infrastructure that's flexible enough to adapt to potentially radical changes in direction every sprint. But I'm getting used to pushing back on the product owner when I see stories that clearly don't fit within the sprint, and that need to be broken down. And it forces me to think in a more modular way, and ultimately results in a more flexible code base.

Now that I've learned how scrum works, one of the most frustrating things for me is when I see the practice being abused. I'm quick to challenge the product owners when they try to introduce a new story in the middle of a sprint. it does happen, and sometimes there are good business reasons for it, but I get annoyed when I see it.

## What I Do About It

Having everybody in the team on the same page is really helpful. I can refer to the definition of done when I don't think something has met my standards, and I can turn to the product owner when people ask me about the status of the features I'm not yet working on. Just knowing who's responsible for what is very helpful.

One of my favorite things about scrum is that I can speak up about the things I don't think are working properly, and see that what I'm saying is actually making a difference. For example, when new stories get forced into the middle of a sprint, I never let that go without raising the issue, and making sure there was a legitimate reason for it to happen.

Because of the retrospectives, I get the opportunity to raise issues that are on my mind—and believe me, I take advantage of those opportunities. Everybody in scrum has an equal voice in terms of how the process works. If I see something that's not going the way I think it should, I can say something and get it addressed. I don't just have to let it happen.

# A Junior Engineer

## Initial Concerns

My role is still pretty new to me, and I'm less experienced working in a team than some of my colleagues are, so I didn't have a clear idea of how scrum was going to be different from any other way of working. When I heard I was going to have to take on stories that were outside of my training, and just push through them and ask for help when I needed it, I was pretty worried. I haven't figured out what my own specialization may be down the road, and it seemed aggressive to expect me to be able to take on stories that deal with aspects of the code I've never even heard of before.

I was especially worried about pairing with people more experienced than I am, and embarrassing myself with stupid mistakes. I also didn't like the idea that I would have to speak up so much. I'm still learning, and I've never been all that outgoing, so it was intimidating.

## What I've Learned

It took a while to get used to the idea that everybody on the scrum team is considered equal. Initially, I didn't like to talk much in meetings. But the scrum rituals encourage everybody to participate, and nobody gets away without saying something. Once I realized that everybody was just as likely to make a mistake if I was, I felt more comfortable saying what was on my mind.

I also really like what I'm learning from working so closely with other engineers. I'm getting exposed to ways of working that I probably wouldn't have figured out until I'd been on the job for a long time. The more we work together, the easier it is for me to take concepts from one part of the code and apply them somewhere else.

I'm also less intimidated now when I'm presented with a story that I don't know how to deal with. The discussion during the sprint planning meeting gives me a chance to hear what more experienced engineers think are the hurdles for any story, so I know what to anticipate. And I know there are people on the team who have the knowledge I need. Working more closely with them gives me a chance to learn how to think outside the textbook cases I've been familiar with.

## What Still Frustrates Me

I'm still scared when I have to take on a story at the top of the backlog that's outside my experience. It's especially frustrating when I see a story I'd like to work on that isn't at the top of the backlog, but that I know I could do better because it's something I'm familiar with. Sometimes I'm tempted to delay work on a story just so I can be in a position to take the story I really want when it becomes available. But I know I'm not supposed to do that, and the scrum master has already called people out on that a few times.

It's also still weird talking so much in the rituals. I think the scrum master might be a little frustrated with me, because I always have to be coaxed to talk. It's especially scary when what I'm thinking doesn't agree with what my manager—or one of the senior engineers—is thinking.

## What I Do About It

I'm learning to be a little bit more open and say what's on my mind more. And knowing I have to say something keeps need more alert, especially when the discussion is about something I'm not familiar with. It forces me to learn things outside my background. And pairing with other, more experienced engineers helps, too. It lets me join in on stories that I'm curious about, but may not have all the skills to do on my own.

Listening to what happens in the planning meetings and during the demos, I've seen that everybody has ideas that turn out to be wrong sometimes. For example, it's very rare that everybody agrees on the number of points to assign to a story during the first vote. Having to justify your position when you're an outlier in the points vote is a great exercise, and it opens up the discussion. It's easy to think that it's just you who doesn't understand. But everybody has things they don't understand. When you participate actively in the discussions, new ideas to come out, and that's a good thing.

# An Engineering Manager

## Initial Concerns

After managing teams for a few years, I was very leery of the idea of a supposedly self-managing team. I've seen the kinds of problems that can come up when people try to work together without adequate supervision, and frequently egos can get in the way of productivity. I've been called into address personnel issues before, and that takes more than an abstract process. And to be honest, it did sound to me as if scrum was trying to replace management with a bunch of buzzwords and fixed procedures.

I was also concerned about how we were going to explain to senior management that we would only be able to estimate roughly when a project would be completed, or even what we were going to produce. Justifying the budget for an engineering team is hard enough when you have fixed deadlines, and can point to specific tangible results. It sounded to me as if scrum was going to take away that justification, leaving me with nothing but open promises.

## What I've Learned

The interesting thing is that the self-managing teams don't actually self manage the way I was expecting. I'm still the manager of the team, and they rely on me for personnel issues, resource allocation, and general leadership. The rest of the company looks to me to take responsibility for what the team is working on, and make sure that what we do coordinates with the needs of the company.

Scrum is about the processes the team follows when it's trying to get work done. Scrum doesn't replace management, but it steps in and provides a pattern that everybody can follow to improve their ability to estimate stories, and make sure everyone is working in a transparent and productive way. I particularly like the way scrum has coordination points between the product group and the engineering group. It takes some of that responsibility off of my shoulders, so I can do the job of managing the team.

And honestly, I like that scrum gives me the opportunity to do some work on the team as a developer again. That's something I've missed as a manager, and I'm glad to get back to it.

## What Still Frustrates Me

Scrum is great within the engineering team, but it would be so much more effective if everybody in the company were on board with it. I sometimes find myself getting caught in the middle, trying to explain the concepts of scrum to people in senior management or on the sales team who want to know that a particular feature can be delivered on a particular date. I mean, I understand why they need that, but it's frustrating having to explain the trade-offs every time.

## What I Do About It

I think we've done a pretty good job of getting most people on board with supporting scrum, and recognizing the value of an iterative process that can respond quickly to changes. I like to explain to people that scrum allows an engineering team to estimate new ideas quickly, and adjust the trajectory of developments to adapt to market changes.

The alternative is coming up with a long-term plan and committing to it, without knowing for sure that it's what the marketplace is going to want. There will always be compromises when it comes to things like that, and that's where people skills are necessary. Most executives would rather have the ability to change direction quickly, since they recognize that things change quickly in web and mobile development—and features that are scheduled too far into the future usually never happen, regardless of what process the team follows.

# A QA Engineer

## Initial Concerns

I wasn't too worried about scrum initially, but then again I didn't think it was going to have much to do with me. My biggest concern was figuring out how I was going to fit into a new process. My work was always pretty well defined, and I didn't want to shake things up. At the end of the day, what I do is important, and I was most concerned that adapting to an agile process was going to mean cutting back on the kind of rigorous testing that I know our products need.

## What I've Learned

It's been interesting participating in the scrum rituals. I didn't have much to say to begin with, but sitting in on the planning meetings gave me a preview of what I was going to have to work on down the road. It also gave me a chance to ask some of the important questions up front. And it turned out that those questions helped the rest of the team make decisions about how they were going to plan out their work. That was an added bonus.

Since I've been integrated into the process, I get to start working on the test suite for a story while it's in development, instead of waiting until afterward. That means the developers don't have to wait as long to get results from my tests, and can make fixes to the code while it's still fresh in their minds.

I also really like the way stories are structured. The acceptance criteria make it clear what aspects to focus on during my testing, and what aspects are just red herrings. And several times I've been able to challenge and modify the acceptance criteria before the team even started working on the story, based on exceptions I could anticipate.

## What Still Frustrates Me

The cadence of scrum still puts a chunk of my work at the end of the line after stories are completed. That means there's usually some concern about getting my tests completed in time for a demo, just to satisfy the expectations of scrum.

I think everyone understands that the scrum deadlines aren't really important to our overall productivity, and that scrum is more about working together efficiently. But I know the team feels better when they can complete all of the stories they've committed to by the end of a sprint. I don't like being the one who makes the team miss those deadlines. But part of that is a function of the type of work I do, not of scrum.

## What I Do About It

Sometimes I have to be the one who reminds people that it's not a real problem if we don't get a story completed in time for a demo. It's much better to do a good job than it is to rush the work just for the sake of scrum points. In fact, rushing to get things done in time for the demo, and working extra hours in order to do it, artificially inflates the velocity of the team. It may show what we can accomplish if we push ourselves, but it isn't in a sustainable manner. It's better to fail at our sprint commitment and get better at estimating than it is to force things to completion in time for an arbitrary demo date. That's what we were taught, although it can be hard to remember sometimes in the excitement of preparing for a demo.

# A Product Manager

## Initial Concerns

The kind of product management I've been used to involves making long-term plans, and working out the details to make sure those plans are realistic. When we started talking about scrum, I felt as if most of what I had been trained to do was going to be thrown out. Scrum felt dismissive of the value of long-term planning.

My organization is responsible for making sure our products will be relevant for years to come, not just for the next two weeks. We have to be able to keep up with competitors, and meet customers' expectations in a predictable way. That can't always happen in two-week increments. I wasn't sure how scrum was supposed to address that.

# What I've Learned

The difference between the product backlog and the sprint backlog clarified a lot of issues for me. I still do my long-range planning, but I do it in the product backlog, where I can nurture ideas that have a long-range potential. It's actually better not setting all of these ideas out in detail. It saves me advance work, since we don't always get to every idea that comes up. But once we know we want to develop something, I can bring it to the top of the product backlog and work it into feature stories that we can bring into the next sprint.

Writing my specifications as stories was tricky at first. I'm not used to thinking in terms of complete slices of functionality. But it's better if I get my head out of the mindset of an engineer, and focus on the benefits we're trying to deliver. When writing stories for the sprints, using the structure we agreed on, I'm able to get just enough detail in to make sure the expectations that are important to me get met. And by playing the role of the customer in the sprint demo, I get to be the one who decides whether or not the work done for the story was acceptable.

# What Still Frustrates Me

Maybe the hardest thing for me was getting my head around the fact that points are relative, and don't have anything to do with the amount of time it's going to take to complete a story. When my management asks me what the team is working on, and the status of features we're planning for the future, they want me to give them specific dates.

The iterative process of scrum generates the kind of data that lets us modify our plan based on the marketplace, but I still feel I lack some control. The fact is we do still have deadlines, and we still have to meet them. There are holidays and other external events that we have to synchronize with. It's just that now we have to deliver whatever's completed.

My management is used to being able to dictate features and timelines months and quarters ahead of time. I find myself explaining the iterative process of scrum over and over again. If I didn't believe in it, and I hadn't seen how well it works, it would be that much harder.

## What I Do About It

The bottom line is the quality of the product. Now that we've gone through several sprints, and I've seen ideas from the product backlog change as a result of data generated through the iterative process of scrum, I have examples to point to that demonstrate the value of this approach. I'm trying to build up more of those examples to help support the argument for scrum going forward.

The ability to coordinate with external deadlines is going to get better over time, I can see that. The more we do this, the better the team gets at estimating how long it'll take to produce a particular new feature. That's the big win for us. When we can estimate more effectively, we'll be in a better position to coordinate our scheduled delivery of features with dates on the calendar. And unlike before, those dates will be a realistic indication of what the team is capable of, and not based on blind hope and brute force.

# A Designer

## Initial Concerns

My biggest concern when I heard we were going to try scrum was the two-week sprint schedule we agreed to. The work I do doesn't always fit into a two-week period, and it usually has to be completed before anybody else can even get started. I didn't want to be the reason the team was less agile, and I was very concerned about having enough time to do the work necessary to provide well-thought-out designs.

At the same time, I wanted to make sure I could be available to the team to produce last-minute assets. I know there's always a need for last-minute assets and quick decisions. Balancing that against the quick turnaround time associated with scrum sounded pretty intimidating.

## What I've Learned

At first I thought I was going to have to be part of the scrum team. The way we're structured, my work sits outside the team, and I act as a resource for them. I work with the scrum master to make sure there's always a queue of tasks for design waiting for me to work on. And thanks to a kanban approach, I can put realistic limits on the number of projects that need to be worked on simultaneously.

The product owner may switch priorities at any point on the items in that queue, so I don't anticipate what I'll be working on next, and that lets me focus on the work at hand. Sometimes the next thing I need to work on is a long-range design plan, and sometimes it's generating assets or reviewing an implementation. It's great to have the opportunity to do some out-of-the-box thinking one day, share my ideas with the product owner, and see the implementation show up in my queue the next day. That almost never happened before we switched to this approach.

I like to attend all of the standups so that I'm on top of what's happening with the team, but I generally attend as an observer, not as a team member. Sometimes I'll follow up with people after the standup to make sure the work is going according to the design plan. When I'm needed, I even get the chance to roll up my sleeves and work side-by-side with the engineers to resolve some flow issue or refine the presentation of an interface. Otherwise, I'm able to focus on the work that's in front of me, knowing that the scrum master will pull into discussions when required.

## What Still Frustrates Me

It never seems to me as if I get enough time to work on long-range planning. Sometimes the features that need to be developed are going to take longer than a sprint or two to design properly.

It can also be a little unsettling having to shift gears without knowing for certain what I'm going to be working on next. I need to be flexible about that so I can support the team and the product most effectively, but I miss being in total control of my day.

## What I Do About It

To be fair, my complaint about lack of long-range design planning isn't any more of a problem now than it was before we started using scrum. At least with scrum I get the opportunity to complain about it every time we have a retrospective. I like to think this keeps the issue top of mind.

Since I'm not officially part of the team, I can work directly with the product owner on ideas that may be longer range than what the team is working on. This gives me the opportunity to do advance planning for design issues that may relate more to the product lifecycle arc then to the next released feature. The approach we're following encourages me to focus my attention on reusable style patterns and guidelines, which can be more versatile than one-off implementation examples.

I also take in a lot of the data the team generates from each iteration of the product. Part of our definition of done includes user acceptance testing, and we're generating interesting statistics about what features the users are taking advantage of, and what doesn't make any sense to them. That helps me focus my work in areas where I know I can add the most value.

# An Executive

## Initial Concerns

I trust the managers I hire. I brought in an engineering manager to make decisions about how to organize the team, and I try not to micromanage that sort of thing. Scrum talks about self-managed teams, and while I like that idea in theory, in practice I've never seen it work. On the other hand, it gets to be overwhelming if managers have to go in and make decisions about every detail in the company. I learned that early on in my career, and even if it's hard sometimes, it's better to be hands-off when it comes to the details of the job.

From all the hype, scrum sounded a little bit too good to be true. I've seen lots of buzzword management initiatives come and go. I was skeptical about the potential for scrum to make the team more flexible while at the same time introducing all these formal processes. I wanted to make sure the engineering managers didn't give the team enough rope to hang themselves. And frankly, I didn't like the sound of adding all these meetings to the calendar.

## What I've Learned

The most surprising thing for me was that the extra meetings actually ended up taking the team away from work less than the meetings we used to have. From what I hear, a lot gets decided in that time, and it's organized really well. We've got a kick-ass scrum master. Our scrum process seems to run like clockwork. And my engineering managers tell me there are fewer personal conflicts on the team, since everybody has a chance to raise issues and get them resolved every sprint.

It's also really great being able to check the scrum board and know immediately what's being worked on, who's doing the work, and where it stands. Before, engineering used to be this black box that I couldn't get a clear picture of without long-drawn-out explanations. And I do understand that nobody wants an executive looking over their shoulder, asking lots of questions when they're trying to do their job. But now I can get all the information I need just by looking at the board and asking the scrum master a few questions.

## What Still Frustrates Me

Looking at the overall picture, I'm getting used to the idea that scrum doesn't add overhead, but it's still something I'm adjusting too. We didn't have a dedicated project manager before, and now the scrum master fills that role. I can see that things wouldn't get done in the same way without somebody to run the process, and I'm impressed with what we've been able to achieve—though I'm still keeping my eye on that bottom line.

And to be perfectly honest, the other thing about scrum that I still need to get used to is that it defines roles for everybody in the engineering organization, but it doesn't seem to have a formal role for me. I don't like being told that my ideas need to be set aside until a new sprint starts, and I'll admit I don't always intend to play by the rules where that's concerned. As the person ultimately responsible for making the decisions about what the company needs to do, I do have insights and ideas that are relevant. I feel that I should be more deeply involved in how engineering works. I always used to be before. I can see that scrum tries to lock me out of that process.

## What I Do About It

When I run the numbers, scrum adds up. Even though it looks like a lot of extra meetings and some extra headcount to manage the process, I can see that the team is getting more work done more efficiently, and people are happier at their jobs. My managers tell me scrum is making their jobs easier, too.

Now that I've seen the process, and watched a few of my ideas filter through onto the scrum board and get delivered at the end of a sprint, I'm getting a little more comfortable with scrum. I miss walking around in engineering and making suggestions based on the big picture, but I've been doing this long enough to know that's an expensive luxury when you're dealing with an engineer's time.

Scrum lets me treat the engineering organization as a resource that I can understand and track with numbers and statistics, and gives me the information I need to understand what everyone in the organization is working on without interrupting them. Ultimately, I need to put my focus on the work being produced, and scrum gives me valuable insight into how long the team is going to be working on the features we need to keep this company going strong.

## Conclusion

This feedback speaks a lot about working through problems that can come up on a scrum team. One of the things we see in many of these comments is that the solutions come from working with people and with the processes that scrum provides. Scrum isn't going to solve all the problems in an organization, and it's not going to address issues that have to do with anything other than the planning and estimation of the work that needs to be done.

Scrum provides the tools and techniques necessary to bring issues to the surface every sprint, and to address these issues before they become standard operating practice. By leveraging the planning that goes into each sprint, and the opportunity to discuss problems and experiment with ways to address them through the retrospective, a team can constantly improve on its own ability to use scrum effectively.

Perhaps the best thing about scrum is that it creates a community of encouragement, based on a mutual understanding of what everybody is working on and how it all fits together. In an effective scrum team, members support each other in maintaining the process and addressing practices that might undermine the scrum team. It's to everybody's advantage to help each other.

CPSIA information can be obtained at www.ICGtesting.com
Printed in the USA
BVOW10s1422140216

436683BV00003B/8/P

9 780994 346919